Information Technology Infrastructure Library

Electronic Data Interchange Message Development Guide

Ray Harris
Roger Till

London: HMSO

Electronic data interchange Message Development Guide

Acknowledgements   CCTA is grateful for the assistance of the Electronic Commerce Association in the preparation of this volume

© Crown Copyright 1996

Applications for reproduction should be made to HMSO's Copyright Unit.

First published 1996

ISBN 0 11 330 843 4

For further information regarding this publication and other CCTA products, please contact:

Customer Services
CCTA
Information Interchange Branch
Rosebery Court
St Andrews Business Park
Norwich
NR7 0HS

Contents

Chapter			Page
	Foreword		9
	Acknowledgements		11
1	**Introduction**		13
	1.1	Background	13
	1.2	Purpose of the guide	13
	1.3	Target readership	13
	1.4	Scope	14
	1.5	Terminology	17
	1.6	Bibliography	17
2	**Starting point**		19
	2.1	Getting Started	19
	2.2	Business case approval	20
	2.3	Processes to be automated	22
	2.4	Data model	23
3	**Reference documents and information sources explained**		25
	3.1	Purpose	25
	3.2	Availability of the documentation	25
	3.3	Documents issued by the UN/ECE	26
4	**How to develop messages**		43
	4.1	General approach and business analysis	43
	4.2	The foundation of UN/EDIFACT design – the syntax rules	52
	4.3	Building a message	55
	4.4	Message implementation guides	77
	4.5	Maintenance	77
	4.6	Multi-format objects	78
	4.7	Interactive EDI (I-EDI)	79
	4.8	Other standards	81

Electronic data interchange Message Development Guide

5		**Security and legal issues**	**83**
	5.1	Security	83
	5.2	Legal	89
6		**Message development examples**	**93**
	6.1	Message examples introduction	93
	6.2	Illustration of a commercial invoice	93
	6.3	Illustration of the single European market declaration message	97
7		**Software development**	**103**
	7.1	The translation process	103
	7.2	Communications management	113
	7.3	Controlling and auditing	119
8		**Testing**	**123**
	8.1	General notes	123
	8.2	Correctness of application data	123
	8.3	Applications interfaces to translation	124
	8.4	Correctness of EDI specification	125
	8.5	Correctness of EDI software	127
	8.6	Correctness of EDI processing	128
	8.7	EDI interface to communications	130
	8.8	Correct functioning of EDI communications channel	130
	8.9	End-to-end testing	132
	8.10	Correctness of the business process – parallel running	132
	8.11	Special note – parallel operation	133
	8.12	Correct functioning of communications control	134
	8.13	Correctness and completeness of archiving and control	134
	8.14	Correctness of automation, reporting and error trapping and recovery	135
	8.15	Log file monitoring	135

9		**Case studies**	**137**
	9.1	Case studies 1: The National Health Service	137
	9.2	Case studies 2: Migration of education proprietary standards to UN/EDIFACT. (MEPS Project)	147

Annex A Glossary 153

Annex B Contacts 159

Annex C STATAC Message 161

Annex D EDI and VAT 171

The requirements regarding computer data interchange of invoice for value added tax purposes in the United Kingdom 171

Bibliography 177

Figures

Figure 1	Example interchange structure	23
Figure 2	Directory message progression	29
Figure 3	Message sequence component of a scenario	47
Figure 4	Message design inputs, outputs, controls and resources	48
Figure 5	Party Information (PARTIN) message	52
Figure 6	The structure of EDIFACT	53
Figure 7	Breakdown by segment of PARTIN message	54
Figure 8	Combination of NAD, CTA and COM segments	67
Figure 9	Combination of NAD, CTA and COM segments with repeats (1)	68
Figure 10	Combination of NAD, CTA and COM segments with repeats (2)	68
Figure 11	Segment grouping (A)	69
Figure 12	Segment grouping (B)	70
Figure 13	A message branching diagram	72
Figure 14	Extract from UNCID rules	90
Figure 15	Example of a paper invoice	94
Figure 16	Example INVOIC message	95
Figure 17	Intrastat form	98
Figure 18	Intrastat branching diagram	99
Figure 19	Intra-EC trade statistics – supplementary declarations	99

Tables

Table 1	SWOT analysis	22
Table 2	An illustration of the layout of the TDED (data elements picked at random)	28
Table 3	Business and information model	44
Table 4	Segment table equivalent of figure 11	70
Table 5	Segment table equivalent of figure 12	70
Table 6	UNS section control	76

Foreword

This volume is part of the CCTA's Information Management Library. The library covers Information Management Data Management, Geographic Information Systems and Information Interchange. The volumes in this library address the effective production, co-ordination, storage, retrieval, dissemination and management of information from internal and external sources in order to improve the performance of an organisation. Information is a valuable resource and its use overall should be effectively managed.

Information Management is not concerned simply with Information Technology. Nor is it the exclusive business of the traditional expert – librarians, records managers, information scientists, data base administrators, traders and so on. Information management is both a policy matter for senior managers and a practical management task for information service professionals and practitioners who have responsibility for its implementation.

The Information Management Library provides guidance on the management of organisations' business-related information. The Library coverage includes Information Management, Data Management, Geographic Information Systems and Information Interchange.

CCTA welcomes customer views on the Information Management Library publications. Please send your comments to:

CCTA
Electronic Commerce Branch
Rosebery Court
St Andrews Business Park
Norwich
NR7 0HS

Acknowledgements

CCTA acknowledges the assistance given by the following organisations in the production of this Guide, and for permission to use materials for case studies and examples:

Perwill Business Solutions
The National Health Service
HM Customs & Excise
The Simpler Trade Procedures Board (SITPRO)
ICI United Kingdom
Enterprise AB

Use of the following trademarks is acknowledged in this document:

Trademark	Owner
IBM	International Business Machines
Tradacoms	Article Number Association
Documentation Manager	EDI-TIE BV, Netherlands
Intersect	SITPRO

1 Introduction

This chapter explains the purpose of the Guide, who should read it and where it sits in the Information Interchange set in the Information Management Library, and describes the structure of the Guide.

1.1 Background

This Guide has been produced to allow IS professionals in government to design UN/EDIFACT messages to enable existing applications to use EDI infrastructures already in place. Other guides in the series detail the business and technical issues surrounding the implementation of EDI systems in government, so this is a logical continuation to that series.

1.2 Purpose of the Guide

The purpose of this Guide is to provide practical information and techniques for successfully designing EDI messages. It will also help the reader to decide whether existing messages can be used, with or without modification, or whether new messages should be designed.

It is assumed that the reader has a level of understanding of EDI such as that provided by the CCTA Information Library publication titled *Electronic Data Interchange in Government: The Business Opportunities*.

1.3 Target Readership

This Guide is aimed primarily at those who will be responsible for designing new EDI messages for EDI enabling existing applications within government departments and agencies:

- IS professionals – managers, analysts and programmers

- Data base professionals – managers, data modellers and implementors.

The Guide may also be of use to EDI partners outside government who need to understand the approach taken by departments and agencies.

It is hoped that the guidelines contained in this Guide will be found to be equally relevant to those starting on EDI message design with no government relationship.

Electronic data interchange Message Development Guide

1.4 Scope

This Guide covers the process of data modelling, the preparation, design and testing of generic UN/EDIFACT messages. The use of supporting documentation is covered in detail to allow the reader to understand the techniques and terminology of UN/EDIFACT and other standards. The reader will also be guided in the process of deciding whether to use existing messages or design new ones, this decision being based on both business and technical criteria.

The chapters of the Guide are laid out in a logical sequence for designing messages:

- Preparation – Chapters 2 and 3

- Practical design issues – Chapters 4, 5, 6, 7 and 8

- Background material – Chapter 9 and Annexes A, B, C, D and E

The individual chapters cover the following topics:

Chapter 1 – Introduction
This chapter explains how the reader can get the most out of *The Guide*. It is a general introduction to explain the content and purpose of the guide

Background – the reason for producing the guide

Purpose of the Guide – what the guide sets out to do

Target Readership – ie programmers and information system managers

Scope – what the Guide covers

Terminology – the conventions used in this publication

Bibliography – the reference documents and further reading.

Chapter 2 – Starting Point
This chapter explains how to get started in message design. It discusses business case approval, deciding which processes need to be automated and how data can be modelled. The chapter uses SSADM terminology to

describe these processes but should be understandable to anyone with a knowledge of structured analysis.

Chapter 3 – Reference Documents and Information Sources Explained
The purpose of this chapter is to provide a description of the important base documents in the UN/EDIFACT process.

Chapter 4 – How To Develop Messages
Initial design activities, message design and message construction are covered in this chapter together with sections on good design techniques and the use of qualifiers. There are further sections covering the migration from other standards to EDIFACT and the standards for binary data and Interactive EDI.

Chapter 5 – Security And Legal Issues
The use of proposed security techniques in UN/EDIFACT and their effect on message design are considered in this chapter.

Chapter 6 – Message Development Examples
This chapter provides examples of the message design process in the real world.

- Example 1 – Purchase Order (ORDERS)

- Example 2 – Single European Market Declaration Message (SEMDEC)

Chapter 7 – Software Development
This chapter will discuss five components affecting EDI message design:

- Communication protocols, eg OFTP, X.400/X.435

- Communications Management, especially when dealing with Value Added Networks

- The translation process, including checking for conformance with various EDI standards

- Data mapping to and from application file formats to include cross-referencing and code list substitution

- Controlling and auditing the entire process, including the tools used to define mapping and EDI messages. This includes debugging options to allow detailed conformance checking of data being sent and received by the user.

Chapter 8 – Testing
This chapter covers the following aspects of testing:

- Generating the verification rules

- Building code-list look-up tables

- Processing the message against the rules and code lists and checking for conformance and exceptions

- Using exception details to pinpoint exact point of failure

- Tracking down to character level if necessary, each stage of the process

- Use of 'bad data' of all types to test error handling and recovery

- Producing the formal test report to identify compliance, or reason for non-compliance.

Chapter 9 – Case Studies
Case studies are chosen from Government's use of EDI to illustrate the techniques discussed in the rest of the publication.

Annex A – Glossary
A comprehensive list of all the abbreviations, acronyms, jargon, manufacturers' terms and idiomatic terms used within the guide.

Annex B – Contacts
A list of useful contacts and addresses including organisation charts where required. This section takes account of the revised structure for developing EDI Standards in the UK and within Europe.

Annex C – STATAC message
A sample of UN/EDIFACT standard message documentation.

Annex D – EDI and VAT
A copy of Customs and Excise rules on the use of invoice information in EDI messages.

Annex E – Bibliography
A list of source documents used in this guide, and further reading.

1.5 Terminology

The Acronyms and terms used in this guide are given in Annex A – Glossary. A few are explained in more detail below, as they are used frequently throughout the guide.

EDI	The exchange of structured data between computer applications. It includes EDIFACT, Tradacoms and ANSI X12 but excludes fax and E-mail.
UN/EDIFACT	Used here to mean the form of EDI formatted according to the rules for United Nations Electronic Data Interchange For Administration, Commerce and Transport – UN/EDIFACT.
UNSM	A United Nations Standard Message, that is, one which has passed through all stages of development and is now stable and available for use.

1.6 Bibliography

Other documents which complement this guide, and which may be useful for future reading, are listed in Annex E.

2 Starting Point

This chapter describes the process of preparing for message design. It does not cover the detail of the planning process and cost-benefit analysis, as these are adequately described in: Electronic Data Interchange in Government: The Business Opportunities, *a companion volume in the Information Management Library series.*

2.1 Getting Started

This guide follows on from two companion volumes in the same series: *Electronic Data Interchange in Government: The Business Opportunities* and *EDI Implementation Guide.* The first volume is aimed at senior business managers and explains what Electronic Data Interchange (EDI) is, and why they should commit resources to it. The second volume is aimed at technical personnel and explains how to implement EDI. This volume, therefore, assumes that EDI is already in use, and that the reader wishes to gain an understanding of the processes required to design customised EDI messages, with a view to improving the efficiency of the EDI enabled business process.

Message design concerns itself with the data to be exchanged between business partners and the standards and convention used by the trading community. This guide concentrates on the United Nations/Economic Commission for Europe rules for Electronic Data Interchange for Administration, Commerce and Transport (UN/EDIFACT) standard as the International Standard for EDI, but the techniques apply to any message standards. The standard to be used will, to some extent, be governed by the trading community to be joined (or established). No assumptions about the carrier mechanism, be it the internet, Value Added Network (VAN) or direct connection, have been made.

EDI allows business, technical or administrative information to be passed from one computer application to another as structured data. The embodiment of that information is the EDI message and so there is a process to convert the business information to a message specification. Just as one would not launch into system design without analysing the problem first or without getting funding, so it is with message design.

Electronic data interchange Message Development Guide

Before starting to design a message a certain amount of preparation is necessary. First of all, the following questions must be answered:

- Is there a business justification for designing a message? If not there is little point in continuing the process. Designing a brand new message can be time and money consuming, so must show a return on the investment

- Is a data model available and is it a true reflection of the business need? Often the model is not available and must be produced. If it is available, it must be relevant for the process being automated. There is little point in designing a message which will not carry the information for which it was designed

- Can the process be automated or will manual intervention be needed (EDI interrupts)? Not all applications lend themselves to EDI and very few can be totally automated but there are generally enough benefits to make EDI worthwhile anyway. What is not acceptable is the need for human intervention in the *middle* of an EDI transaction such that errors and/or delays can be introduced into the process

- Does the planned trading partner or community already use EDI? If so to which standards? Any messages already in use by the partner or within the community, which might meet the business requirement, should be considered before designing new ones. The potential partners' requirements should also be taken into account when designing a message.

2.2 Business Case Approval

The guide *Electronic Data Interchange in Government: The Business Opportunities* deals with the benefits of EDI in general, but the benefits of designing messages are more difficult to quantify. A custom-designed message is like a bespoke suit: a necessity if nothing exists which fits or meets the requirements, but a luxury if an off-the-peg version meets all needs. The benefit of the custom message is its perfect fit to the business requirement. The rest of this section discusses the steps required to decide if that benefit is sufficient to justify the time and cost involved.

Message design is a technical process, which is reflected in this guide, but it does require a good understanding of the business process being automated. Message design can be costly, so it is important to try to reuse what already exists. The options for supporting a transaction should be considered, and the most cost justified route adopted.

Assuming that there is a requirement to transfer information between two applications, and that UN/EDIFACT is the preferred technique for the interchange of data representing that information, then the following points need to be taken into account:

- Does an existing UN/EDIFACT Standard Message (UNSM) meet the requirements exactly?

- Does an existing UN/EDIFACT draft Message meet the requirements exactly?

- Could an existing UN/EDIFACT message be modified to meet the requirements?

- Is there an existing UN/GTDI (United Nations Guidelines for Trade Data Interchange) or Tradacoms message which meets the requirements with or without modification?

- Does any other form of EDI have a message or data set which could meet the requirement?

- Do none of the above apply?

The cost of designing EDI messages increases from zero if a suitable UNSM exists, to a maximum if a message must be designed from scratch. There are circumstances other than cost to be taken into account though, when making the business case. Below is a simple Strengths, Weaknesses, Opportunities and Threats (SWOT) analysis of the general case of modify versus design. By changing this for a particular case and weighting the results, it can be decided which technique best suits a particular application.

	Modify Existing Message	**Design New Message**
Strengths	Most of the groundwork is already done. Changes are usually easier to implement	Fits business requirement exactly. Can be very specific to requirement and thus efficient.
Weaknesses	May not fit business requirement exactly. Message might be so generic as to be difficult to understand and use effectively.	Cost to design and implement can be high. Time from conception to it becoming an acceptably stable message can be very long. Software providers may have difficulty supporting it if not a UNSM
Opportunities	Other users may require similar changes.	The world might be holding its breath for just such a message. Other users may help get it through the overall acceptance process.
Threats	Existing message users may object to changes, and block them in UN/EDIFACT.	If the message is too specific or overlaps an existing message too much, there will be difficulties getting it accepted by a large group of users.

Table 1: SWOT Analysis

The message designer also needs to consider if the message is a candidate to be a UNSM or whether it can be proprietary. Simply put, if the message is for internal use only, will always be so, and will work with existing translators, then the costs of making it a standard message far outweigh the benefits. In real life though, the above rarely applies.

2.3 Processes To Be Automated

Business Information Modelling (BIM), using a structured analysis and design methodology, such as SSADM (Structured Systems Analysis & Design Methodology) for a process, enables the logical process design and the logical data design to be identified and document flow diagrams, data flow diagrams and entity

Chapter 2
Starting Point

models to be produced. The BIM technique described in 4.1.2, does not specify a particular methodology, but is applicable to most modern structured analysis.

This document assumes a familiarity with structured analysis, but if a deeper knowledge of SSADM is required, contact the CCTA for their recommendations, or see *Structured Systems Analysis and Design Methodology* by G Cutts.

The entity model shows the relationships between the processes and the data entities. The process outline identifies the processes, or business functions, to be automated, also the data entities affected can be determined from an entity function matrix.

If the process outline shows that manual input or action is required for a process to continue at any point, then either the process can be only partially automated, or the business process might be in need of re-engineering.

2.4 Data Model

To be considering transferring data between applications in EDIFACT format, the designer must know the type of data to be transferred and be able to model it in terms of an EDIFACT message.

The largest unit of information in EDIFACT is the Interchange. An Interchange is an envelope for, normally, several messages. These are usually logically related, as part of the same transaction for example, but may be independent entities which, it happens, are being transferred to the same recipient. As such the interchange is of little concern to the reader at present.

Interchange header	EDI Message	EDI Message	EDI Message	Interchange trailer

Figure 1: Example Interchange Structure

The next level down is the message, and it is this level and below which concerns this guide. The message, or transaction set in ANSI parlance, contains only logically related data and has a specific function, such as an invoice or purchase order. The message is analogous to the paper form that it normally replaces. Care should be taken, though, that the message is not just a translation of the paper form, as this can lead to the propagation of inbuilt inefficiencies.

A model of the activities and the data required to fulfil those activities needs to be produced. SSADM Current Physical Data Flow Diagrams model existing paper based systems to show how documents flow between sources and destinations. These serve as the basis for constructing the Required Logical Data Flow Diagram, which shows what the system is required to accomplish. Data flow diagrams show various views of the data in a system. The one which interests the reader is the Required Physical Data Flow, derived from the Required Logical Data Flow, which shows how the required message will be implemented.

The entity model shows the relationships between the business functions and the data entities. The data entities passed between external systems are the messages. Normalisation of these entities produces simple tables from the complex data structures. Whereas in classical systems this would lead to the database design, here it should lead on to message design. In very simplistic terms the tables map to segments and the lines in the tables map to composite data elements, so the basic building blocks have been identified prior to design work starting. Be prepared, however, to be pragmatic and revisit this model when mapping to existing EDI data objects. Sub-optimal data design is preferable to the cost and time of designing, and submitting for standardisation, new EDI objects. Case study 2 examines a set of messages which were designed wholly from existing EDIFACT data objects.

3 Reference Documents and Information Sources Explained

This chapter identifies the important documents that are relevant to the design of EDI messages in UN/EDIFACT format. It indicates which documents are important, eg containing rules, and those which may be only useful in certain circumstances. The owners of the documents are identified and where the documents may be obtained, if deemed necessary.

3.1 Purpose

The purpose of this chapter is to provide the prospective message designer with a complete list of documents on which UN/EDIFACT message design is based. It should be noted that it should not be necessary to obtain and read all of these documents. The essentials of message design are clearly explained in Chapter 4 of this document. However, there are certain documents that must be obtained, e.g. directories of the latest messages' formats and their components. Other documents may only be of interest in certain circumstances. However, it is important to know that they are available and from whom.

3.2 Availability of the documentation

3.2.1 Documentation Sources

The majority of the documentation described in this chapter is issued by the United Nations Economic Commission for Europe (UN/ECE). Nevertheless, most of the documents have been brought together in one handy set, called The EDIFACT Service, issued and maintained by the Simpler Trade Procedures Board (SITPRO). However, with the break-up of SITPRO it is not clear what will happen to this publication. For the best advice on the availability in the UK of these sources of information, the reader is recommended to contact the Electronic Commerce Association. However, for readers with World Wide Web access the following Universal Resource Locators (URL) could be useful:

http://www.eca.org.uk – for general EDI information
http://www.unicc.org/unece/trade/untdid for UN/ECE documents

Electronic data interchange Message Development Guide

http://www.itu.ch – for ITU and UN/ECE documents
http://www.iso.ch – for ISO documents
http://www.premenos.com – for general EDI, ANSI and UN/ECE information.

3.2.2 Documentation Tools

Many of the source documents listed below are available electronically, either for reference (eg SITPRO's EDIFACT Service) or for use in message documentation (eg EDITIE's Documentation Manager, SITPRO's Intersect). The use of one of these documentation tools is recommended. These tools come with some or all of the current directories, so enabling the designer to choose the relevant directory for the proposed message. The designer may have no choice if the trading partner is committed to a particular directory, otherwise the most current directory should be used.

By having the segment, composite data element and simple data element definitions at hand, the work of the message designer is simplified. Having designed the message, existing elements can be grouped as necessary, moved around within the message definition and finally printed out in the UN's standard format. The tools generally allow new directories to be added using the UN/EDIFACT DIRDEF format, or a proprietary file format.

3.3 Documents issued by the UN/ECE

It should be noted that, because EDIFACT was born at the UN/ECE, it is called UN/EDIFACT by that organisation. It is, however, commonly referred to as EDIFACT, ie without the UN prefix. In this document both are used; UN/EDIFACT in relation to UN/ECE documentation (to observe the proprieties) and EDIFACT otherwise. The terms are, essentially, interchangeable.

The UN/ECE 'issue' two prime documents, the Trade Data Elements Directory (TDED) and the Trade Data Interchange Directory (TDID). The word 'issue' is in quotes because in paper format the TDED is issued only rarely. The TDID consists of a number of separate documents, some fairly static and some reissued twice a year. There is no single publication of the full TDID.

New documents are approved at bi-annual meetings of the UN/ECE, Working Party 4, Group of Experts 1 (WP.4/GE.1).

3.3.1 The Trade Data Elements Directory

When a data element is required and there is not one listed for the requisite function in the UN/EDIFACT directory (qv), then the TDED should be a prime source.

The TDED contains three volumes of information, with Volume I being 95% of the document. The parts are:

- Volume I – Standard Data Elements

- Volume II – User Code List

- Volume III – Compendium of Trade Facilitation Regulations.

Volume I is the major source of information. It has to be remembered, however, that the data elements contained in this volume have their sizes constrained by the size of boxes on forms. There is no such constraint in EDI. Data elements are identified in the directory by a four numeral key. It is a structured key which categorises each data element. This convention has been carried through into the UN/EDIFACT data element directory. As the latter is one of the most important source documents, a full explanation of the key and directory contents is described under the TDID section below. See Table 2 for an abstract from the TDED.

Volume II contains some code lists relating to international trade. The codes are useful to EDIFACT users as most of the UN/EDIFACT data elements carry coded values. The need to know of these particular codes becomes apparent when they are referenced by the EDIFACT code lists (see below).

Volume III contains particular recommendations relating to international trade procedures and processes. These recommendations are very unlikely to be of interest to message designers.

Electronic data interchange Message Development Guide

5118	Price	E 91.2
Desc:	The monetary value associated with a purchase or sale of an article, product or service.	
Repr:	n..15	
5377	**Price change indicator, coded**	E S.93A
Desc:	Indication of the type of price change for a line item (e.g. increased).	
Repr:	an..3	
Note:	User or association defined code. May be used in combination with 1131/3055	
5379	**Price/tariff type, coded**	E 93.2
Desc:	Specification of type of price or tariff calculation used for products.	
Repr:	an..3	

Table 2: An Illustration of the Layout of the TDED (data elements picked at random)

Notes: Representation is explained in 3.3.4.1
E 93.2 is UN/EDIFACT directory 1993 version 2 (3.3.2.2)

3.3.2 The Trade Data Interchange Directory

The TDID is stated by the UN/ECE to be made up of the following documents:

- the syntax rules (ISO 9735)

- the UN/EDIFACT data element directory

- the UN/EDIFACT code sets

- a directory of composite data elements

- a directory of segments

- a directory of United Nations Standard Messages

- syntax implementation guidelines

- message design guidelines

- uniform rules of conduct for interchange of trade data by Teletransmission

- other explanatory material.

3.3.2.1 *The syntax rules*
The syntax rules are those for EDIFACT. The rules are described in more detail later under 'ISO documentation'.

3.3.2.2 *Directories*
Data directories are central to the design of EDI messages. The UN/EDIFACT directories of messages, segments, composite data elements, simple data elements and code lists have been issued twice a year on diskette as a general rule. Thus, in 1995 there was issued the 95A and the 95B directory sets. Obviously, the reason for the continual issue of directory sets is that each new set has additions, deletions and changes from the previous version. (The A and B used to be numeric – see Table 2 above.)

To establish what version of a message is being used, UN/EDIFACT messages refer to the directory set that contains their details and components. This is explained in full in the section on 'version and release' later. The layout of the data element directory is similar to that of the TDED described above (Table 2).

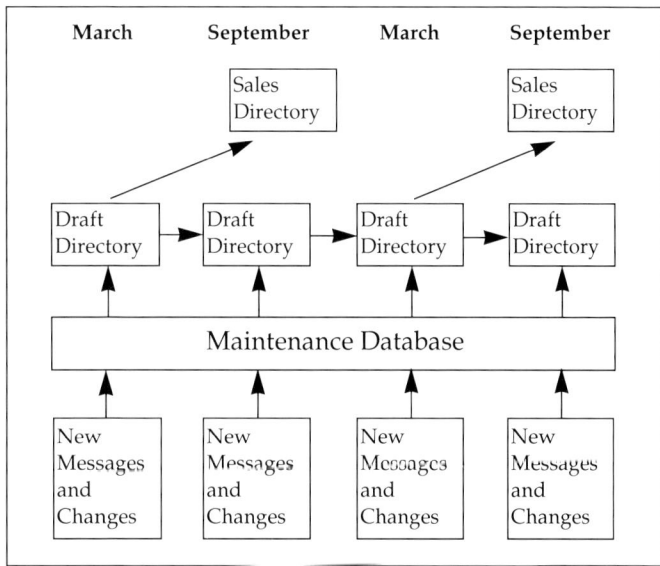

Figure 2: Directory Message Progression

Figure 2 indicates how the directories have been organised to enable new messages, and changes to old messages, to be incorporated into the UN/EDIFACT process. The structure of any particular version of a message is, therefore, related to a directory issue which is quoted in the message header.

While it is recognised that messages structured from past directories should use the version/release rules appropriate to whichever of those directories is used, in this document it is assumed that message designers will want to use the latest directories. The current conventions used for version and release purposes are explained in the section on syntax. It is important to understand that when a message enters a draft or standards directory, it will remain there even if it is not modified in any way. Thus, look in the latest directory for the particular message structure required.

Notwithstanding the information above, **it is believed that the system of directory progression will change in the near future (1996/7)**. There is a strong movement to standardise on two UN/EDIFACT directories per year. These will not be 'draft' or 'standard' but will simply be 'UN/EDIFACT directories'. This will simplify the directory progression issue.

In UN/EDIFACT, when messages are being developed, they go through a status progression that then makes them eligible to be accepted into the appropriate directories. The kinds of status, currently, are:

- Status 0

- Status 1

- Status 2.

Status 0
For a message to be given the level of Status 0, it has to consist of what is called the 'boilerplate'. This means essentially full message documentation. It does not, though, need to go through detailed technical conformance assessment before it is accepted by WP.4/GE.1.

Status 1
When a message has, within the UN/ECE process, reached a reasonable level of stability, it can be submitted for Status 1 acceptance. To achieve this attribute it has to pass independent technical assessment and be acceptable to all UN/EDIFACT geographical regions. After acceptance it can be included in the (normally) following draft directory issued by WP.4/GE.1.

Status 2
Status 2 is requested for a message when it is considered to be in a stable state and, therefore, will have few amendments made to it in the future. It can then be placed into the standards directory.

Having described the current process regarding the various stages that a message can go through in the UN/EDIFACT process, it must be stated that, in conjunction with changes in the frequency of production of directories, ie the 'disappearance' of the 'draft' and 'standard' tags, **there are, logically, moves afoot to abolish the Status 1 and Status 2 gradings.**

3.3.3 Interactive EDI

Interactive EDI is fairly new on the UN/EDIFACT scene. Further information on its function is given under the heading syntax under 'ISO documentation'. However, it is becoming recognised that its requirements in relation to message structures are somewhat different from those of 'batch' messages.

There is a pilot interactive EDI (I-EDI) directory detailed in UN/ECE document TRADE WP.4/R.1139 Add.5. It appears that I-EDI will, at least for short term, have its own directory set – that is until the requirements are fully recognised. Eventually it is expected that efforts will be made to merge this directory set with the more mature one of the batch messages.

3.3.4 Data element tags

The convention for structuring data element tags is important to message designers, as they will wish to keep a directory of their data elements. That directory will probably contain a mixture of current UN/EDIFACT data elements and those created by the designers where there are no UN/EDIFACT data

Electronic data interchange Message Development Guide

elements available. The following is, therefore, a useful convention to follow.

The format of a UN/EDIFACT data element tag is structured as follows:

Group 1: (0001–0799) Service data elements; (1000-1799) documentation, references:
Data elements intended for data handling or documentation purposes, such as those required to service the interchange of user data, document and message names, references and reference numbers, ordinal numbers, eg item and page numbers, number of copies of documents;

Group 2: (2000–2799) Dates, times, periods
All expressions of time, such as calendar dates, periods of time (month, week, day), time limits, commencement and expiry dates;

Group 3: (3000–3799) Parties, addresses, places, countries
Names and addresses of legal and physical persons, designations of officials, organisational units, places, countries, routes;

Group 4: (4000–4799) Clauses, conditions, terms, instructions
Authentications, authorisations, endorsements, certificates, clauses, conditions, terms, reference clauses, stamps, labels, requests, instructions, receipts, statements, information texts;

Group 5: (5000–5799) Amounts, charges, percentages
Financial values, amounts, charges; other quantities and values for commercial, transport, customs, statistical and any other purposes; other details, such as prices, rates, percentages and discounts, used as a basis for invoice calculations, etc;

Group 6 (6000–6799) Measure identifiers, quantities (other than monetary)
Dimensions, weights, volumes, distances, temperature, currency, other quantities, with the exception of monetary quantities in Group 5, measure unit specifiers;

Chapter 3
Reference Documents and Information Sources Explained

Group 7 (7000–7799) Goods and articles; descriptions and identifiers
Descriptions, classifications and identification of goods and articles, consignment identifiers, number and kind of packages, dangerous goods details;

Group 8 (8000–8799) Transport modes and means, containers
Identification and description of means of transport and containers, transport equipment details, transport modes and movements, voyage and flight numbers;

Group 9 (9000–9799) Other data elements
Data elements not belonging to any of the specific categories 1–8.

It will be noted that each group does not cover a full 1000 tags, ie it ends at n799 (where n is the group number). This is because the second digit is of special significance. The UN/EDIFACT secretariat allocates tags up to n699 for entry in the directories. Tags from n700 to n799 are used in message types under development eg status 0. Tags from n800 upwards are for free use. This is, of course, very useful for developers of new messages using the above categories (and this is recommended) as it indicates which data elements have been accepted by UN/EDIFACT and which have not. Further conventions for tagging data elements are detailed in Chapter 4.

3.3.4.1 Data element representation
A further convention which has been carried down from the TDED and is used in UN/EDIFACT directories is that relating to the representation of the format of data elements. This is:

a	alphabetic characters
n	numeric characters
an	alphanumeric characters
a3	3 alphabetic characters, fixed length
n3	3 numeric characters, fixed length
an3	3 alphanumeric characters, fixed length
a..3	variable length, maximum 3, alphabetic characters
n..3	variable length, maximum 3, numeric characters
an..3	variable length, maximum 3, alphanumeric characters

Electronic data interchange Message Development Guide

It is important that these conventions are used in message documentation as part of the documentation conventions of UN/EDIFACT. This enables new readers to understand the messages without lengthy interpretation of the documentation standards used. For those message designers who wish to maintain their directories in precisely the same format as the UN/ECE documentation, TRADE/WP.4/R.1023/Rev.2 details 'UN/EDIFACT Rules for Presentation of Standardised Message and Directories Documentation' in electronic and hard copy formats.

3.3.5 Syntax implementation guidelines

The syntax implementation guidelines were issued to help understand and use the syntax rules which, like many international standards, can be quite difficult to understand. The implementation guidelines have not been amended since they were first issued, although the syntax rules have. It is considered that there is little worth in bothering with the implementation guidelines unless they are updated and reissued in relation to the next version of the syntax to be released.

3.3.6 Message design guidelines

The UN/EDIFACT message design guidelines – TRADE/WP.4/R.840/Rev.2 – is an important document. The current version is regarded by many people as not being a very good document – it mixes up rules with UN/EDIFACT procedural issues, for example. However, the guidelines are used as a basis for UN/EDIFACT message design, and as a prime document for message conformance assessment. A revised set of rules should be issued in 1996–7.

Interactive EDI has its own set of guidelines for interactive messages. These are in an embryo state currently and have been issued as part of the documentation relating to a pilot trial of I-EDI messages. It is expected that an approved copy will be issued during 1996.

3.3.7 The UNCID rules

The Uniform Rules of Conduct for Interchange of Trade Data by Teletransmission are better known as the UNCID rules. They relate in a semi-legal way to how EDI should be conducted between data exchange partners. They have now been overtaken by the work on

Chapter 3
Reference Documents and Information Sources Explained

		Interchange Agreements and other legal aspects. In this respect, see Chapter 5, Security And Legal Issues.
3.3.8	Other UN/ECE documentation	Each year in March and September WP.4/GE.1 meets to consider papers submitted by members. Some of those documents, although approved by the Group, have not found their way into TDED. They are, however, pertinent to message design.
3.3.9	Message version/release rules	These rules are set out in UN/ECE paper TRADE/WP.4/R.601 dated 31 July 1989 and in R.720 dated 14 December 1990. Incidentally, R.601 also contains rules for subsetting messages, see below. Because every UN/EDIFACT message structure has a parent directory in which it and its components can be found, it is necessary, when transmitting a message, to be able to identify the directory so that the message's structure is unambiguous to any translation software that has to deformat it. This information goes into the header of the message and is quoted in message documentation.
3.3.10	Message documentation format	It is vital that the layout of EDI message documentation when using UN/EDIFACT is the same for all messages. The reasons are obvious. It makes the documentation easier to read for those who need to know about the messages, eg translation software installers, trading partners and technical conformance assessors. Furthermore, following a conventional layout helps to ensure completeness of the documentation. Document TRADE/WP.4/R.1023/Rev.2 details the 'UN/EDIFACT Rules for Presentation of Standardised Message and Directories Documentation' in hard copy and electronic formats. Chapter 6, Message Development Examples, contains an example of a UN/EDIFACT message that can be used as a template for other message document formats.
3.3.11	Subsets	UN/EDIFACT messages contain the total requirements of the international community, normally going beyond the requirements of any individual user. It was found that users, especially within a single industry, were getting together to define subsets of the UN/EDIFACT messages. The UN/ECE understands this move as one which is, in the circumstances, wholly reasonable. However, to avoid

Electronic data interchange Message Development Guide

a deterioration of the standards work already done, a set of rules was formulated as to the structure of a subset in relation to its parent message. These rules are set out in document TRADE/WP.4/R.601 issued in September 1989 (the same document contained version/release rules described above). The subset rules are important to message designers as, among other things, they help to avoid complications for EDIFACT message translators. The following are the rules for taking a subset of a UN/EDIFACT message – they are also quite relevant to any message based on the EDIFACT standards and possibly other standards.

It has to:

- have the same function as the parent message

- contain all mandatory groups and segments and the mandatory data elements within them

- keep the same status, order and content of the required groups, segments etc

- have no additions

- contain the same information as the parent message in the message header (addition is allowed).

(Chapter 4 – How To Develop Messages, explains the above terminology.)

3.3.12 Message implementation guides

The UN/ECE does not produce implementation guides. Nevertheless, it is known that the Technical Assessment Group (TAG) of the Western European EDIFACT Board has accepted a proposal, from EWOS (the European Workshop for Open Systems), to produce a document setting out the rules for writing message implementation guides (contents and format). Until this becomes available, the best bet is to get hold of a good, relevant document, eg the UK EDIFACT Trade Message Convention that has had input from a number of industries and other sources, and copy its layout etc.

Chapter 3
Reference Documents and Information Sources Explained

3.3.13 TAG checklists — The Technical Assessment Checklist's prime use is for technical assessment groups to have a single formal document on which to base message conformance to document layout, syntax and message design guidelines. There is a separate checklist for batch and interactive messages. The documents could be useful to a message designer, possibly to confirm, or otherwise, an unclear understanding. However, most message designers do well enough without them.

3.3.14 Locodes — Locodes are location codes for ports in international trade. Understandably, it is a very large document. It may be useful to use certain codes depending upon the type of message involved (eg in international trade).

3.3.15 Business Information Modelling (BIM) — There has been no formally approved documentation issued by the UN/ECE on how to model messages. However, there is a BIM Group that has issued a 'Business and Information Modelling Framework for UN/EDIFACT'. This is gradually being accepted as the correct approach to message design.

3.3.16 ISO documentation — There are two documents that were initially written in the UN/ECE and which have been successfully turned into standards issued by the International Organization for Standardization (ISO). These are:

- the UN/EDIFACT syntax rules which are ISO 9735

- the Trade Data Interchange Directory which is ISO 7372.

3.3.16.1   ISO 9735
The EDIFACT syntax rules are the grammar of the messages. All have to conform to the rules.

The syntax defines the way components of message structures are placed together into logical groups (composite data elements, segments and segment groups). This will be explained in more detail in Chapter 4.

Also included in the EDIFACT syntax are special logical groups of data called 'service segments'. These are in the form of headers and trailers to messages, groups of messages (functional groups) and interchanges. In terms of message design there is no need to be concerned with any of the service segments except for the message header and the message trailer. The way these two segments are used will be set out in Chapter 4. However, to show the context of the usage of messages (Figure 5), Party Information (PARTIN) message.

The current version of ISO 9735 is version 3. Version 4 of the syntax is under consideration by the UN/ECE. It has in it some major changes. It should be approved by the UN/ECE and passed to ISO for consideration in 1996. Thereafter, it could take at least a year, but most likely two, before it is accepted as ready for issue by the appropriate ISO committee. The results are quite likely to have an impact on message structures and, therefore, on message design.

3.3.16.2   ISO 7372

ISO 7372 covers the main part of the TDED, that relating to the data directory. There are a number of UN/ECE recommendations that are in TDED that are not covered. However, for all practical purposes for EDI they are the same. In substance, ISO 7372 is simply a cover sheet for parts of the TDED. Therefore, anyone wishing to buy a copy is as well going directly to the UN/ECE.

3.3.17 Joint ISO and UN documentation

The main joint work project between the UN/ECE and ISO is the Basic Semantic Repository (BSR) project. The project will define Basic Semantic Units (BSU's) and Bridges. The objective of the project is defined as:

To establish an operational BSR which will provide end users with the facilities they need for linking their data representations in existing EDI directories.

A BSU is:

A concept unambiguously defined and applicable in one or more contexts in an EDI environment. It may be part of a broader concept in which case it shall possess at least all the characteristics of that concept.

A Bridge is:

The link between a BSU and its related unit(s) of information in a given directory.

Thus, in a nut shell, the project will define BSU's, each of which will be linked to a data element in a number of different EDI data directories. It will thus be theoretically possible to obtain equivalencies between data elements in different directories, at least at a conceptual level.

The project has not been in existence very long (in standardisation terms!). There is a great deal of work to do. However, in that the data dictionary is the most important document of all, the outcome of this project should be of interest to all message designers, especially to those who are designing cross industry messages. It is a well intentioned move to enable users to standardise on the descriptions of the data they exchange.

3.3.18 Other documentation and information sources

CCTA – The CCTA has produced the following documents:

Electronic Data Interchange in Government: The Business Opportunities;
EDI Implementation Guide.

The first volume should not offer a lot to the reader of this guide as its contents are aimed at business managers. The second document contains a great deal of useful information which, although not of direct concern to the EDI message designer, could be a very useful reference manual.

Documents on security and on legal aspects are under development.

CEN – the Comité Européen de Normalisation (Committee for European Standardisation) has approved ISO 9735 and ISO 7372 (see above) as European Standards and issued them as EN 29735 and EN 27372 respectively. There is no need to try to obtain this documentation from CEN as it is easier to obtain it elsewhere, eg through the British Standards Institution (payment required) or the UN/ECE.

SITPRO – the Simpler Trade Procedures Board, was a prime source of EDIFACT documentation and, in particular, issued a set of volumes called 'The EDIFACT Service' that contained many of the documents referred to above, plus advice on EDI. The EDIFACT Service has also been updated every six months with the latest directories. However, it has been decided that the EDI standards and software sections of SITPRO shall be removed from that organisation. Thus the future of The EDIFACT Service hangs in the balance.

ECA – The Electronic Commerce Association (formerly the EDI Association) has been set up to help EDI users, both new and old. It has a number of industry groups working, mainly, on message construction. It is a useful source of documentation and advice. Although it does not currently produce any official documents, its membership constitutes an enormous amount of knowledge on EDI and messaging. It has a Public Service Interest Section covering central and local government and education.

ANA – The Article Number Association's main responsibility in EDI is for the TRADACOMS standards. These were based on early work in the UK and are nearly equivalent to the Guidelines for Trade Data Interchange, the UN/ECE recommendation for EDI that has now been replaced by EDIFACT. The ANA works, largely, in the general trade area (supermarkets, general consumer goods). Recognising the advance of EDIFACT, the ANA issues a UK EDIFACT Trade Message Convention which maps its prime TRADACOMS messages into EDIFACT being a subset of the relevant UN/EDIFACT messages. This is a useful document for the EDI users who are interested in that area (invoice, purchase order, price catalogue etc), particularly as it has had input from a wider range of industries than is normally associated with the ANA.

IBM (Germany) – This company has, for a number of years, produced and distributed freely a small booklet containing a list of messages going through the UN/EDIFACT process, ie Status 0, Status 1 and Status 2. The stated function and principles of each message listed is also given. This is a very useful source of information when looking, for example, to see whether a message has been designed for any particular function. If it is required, try the ECA first.

BSI – The British Standards Institution sells UK standards. This includes ISO 9735 and ISO 7372. It is also the source for other documentation that may be useful to EDI users, eg lists of country codes, ISO 6523 Structure for the Identification of Organisations and Organisation Parts (it also has the register for these).

UKCEDIS – The UK Confederation for EDI Standards was set up by five organisations (the ANA, the EDIA (now ECA), APACS, SITPRO and BINA) interested in EDI standardisation. Although it does not currently produce any official documents, its membership constitutes an enormous amount of knowledge on EDI. Most members will either know the answer to a problem or be able to point to the appropriate expert.

4 How To Develop Messages

The purpose of this chapter is to provide the EDI message designer with enough information to enable UN/EDIFACT messages to be designed. It takes a logical approach in detailing how to start the process by collecting the relevant information and applying modelling techniques. It then covers the UN/EDIFACT structures and the message design rules in detail. This is followed by good practice advice and maintenance aspects. Finally, it covers the use of EDIFACT for assisting in the transmission of other objects (eg graphs and drawings) and some thoughts on interactive EDI messaging.

4.1. General Approach and Business Analysis

4.1.1 General

This chapter assumes that a decision has been made to move from what was, most likely, a paper form based transfer of information, to one of direct computer application to computer application exchange. The easy way would probably be to take all the items of data on the form and send them in a file of records in a fixed format. In fact, this was how the first EDI was sent. Experience has shown that this is, in the vast majority of cases, not cost effective in the medium and long term. For this reason there has been a great deal of effort expended to find a more flexible and yet efficient means of formatting data when it is transferred. This means abiding by message design rules that may seem a nuisance in a particular circumstance but which in the long term are beneficial to all.

4.1.2 Business Analysis

The Business and Information Modelling (BIM) activity of UN/EDIFACT provides the following framework on which to base the message design work:

	Information	Activity
Business Analysis	Business Object Classes 2	Functions Entity Types and Data Flows 1
EDI Requirements	EDI Message Data 4	EDI Supported Activities (Scenarios) 3
UN/EDIFACT Message Design	UN/EDIFACT Messages Structures 6	UNSM Purpose and Scope 5

Table 3: Business and Information Model

(Note: UNSM in box 5 is United Nations Standard Message.)

Thus, rather than leap into a proprietary, albeit pragmatic, solution, a more formal and considered approach is necessary. This means taking a step back and fully understanding what is being attempted. This rearward step and the new view it gives is an important step in order to get a wider, non-blinkered picture of the best options for the future.

It is, therefore, worthwhile considering the move to EDI as part of a larger process of upgrading. It is particularly important that the benefits of EDI are secured and thought must be given to the fact that data is received quicker. There is, also, a greater predictability about it in terms of lessening errors and timing. This may affect message design.

The timing of the transmission of a message is likely to be different from that of posting a document. Leaving transmission to the last moment – because there is no need to worry about postal delays – means that the data is less likely to have to be amended. However, that has to be viewed in the light of the recipient's requirements who may feel that one benefit of EDI is earlier receipt of the information. Thus, message design does not only involve the sender but, also, the recipient. It is as well that exchange partners co-operate to the full in message design (and on other aspects) so that both/all can optimise their benefits.

In short, the first activity of message design is to look at the broad trading or administrative business requirement in co-operation with the proposed EDI partner or partners, and then narrow it down to the more specific requirements of the 'sub-function'. This is the main focus of the proposed EDI activity.

A model of the activities and the data required to fulfil those activities can be produced. The first effort would be very broad and simplistic while the second would be more detailed but not yet to the level required to start designing a specific message. For example, the results would show the areas of potential EDI activity (box 1 in Table 3) and what functions (receiving, amending, paying etc.) are likely to be successful candidates for data exchange. It would also show the relationship between the objects (box 2 of Table 3) which are involved in the process, eg supplier, order, product, customer.

4.1.3 EDI requirements

Once the high level model has been agreed, the next stage is to look at the data required (box 4 of Table 3) and the activities supported (box 3 of Table 3.)

Readers will note the use of the term 'scenarios' in box 3 of the BIM model. It is not yet clear (an ISO committee ISO/IEC JTC1 SC30 may make it so in due course) exactly what a scenario is. In most people's minds it seems to relate to a complete business case. That is to say, all the EDI requirements that are needed to undertake EDI in a specific area, eg tourism or construction. The support of a particular scenario, therefore, means support of its components such as messages, security standards, legal agreements etc.

The Data
At this point in the process, it should be apparent what broad functions are to be supported by EDI. These can then be broken down into sub-functions. If invoicing is the broad function then this can be sub-divided into, for example, payment terms, delivery details and price

Electronic data interchange Message Development Guide

information. A complete list of the sub-functions should be kept with an indication of broad activity or activities to which they are appropriate. An important aspect of EDI is data reusability. This not only refers to single items of data but to logical groups of data objects. It should be determined which of the sub-functions are mandatory within a broad function.

The next step is to determine exactly what data is required in each sub-function defined in the dictionary.

In the vast majority of cases this will be equivalent to the information printed on some form of document or even as sent in an 'old fashioned' file/record based format. In fact, some of the sub-functions may be equivalent to a box or an area on a form, however, it is not necessarily so. Full consideration must be given to what is really required to be transferred, for example, most business and administrative documents consist of structured forms. These forms normally have data pre-printed on them, e.g. sender name and address, VAT number and telephone and facsimile details. Some hard copy documents are sent containing information that is not actually needed by the recipient – but that is how they have been completed for years!

The data derived from the current documentary processes needs to be compared with the 'top down' requirements resulting from the modelling process. It may be that there is not a one-to-one equivalence of broad functions from the modelling process and documents in the current 'real world'. If not, the reasons why should be investigated, but overall the results of the modelling process should determine the final goal.
In defining the data requirements of all of the broad functions it should be noted for each one which items are mandatory. All these data objects can then be brought together to form a data object dictionary. The essence of efficient EDI is the requirement of data to perform with exactly the same result within different broad and/or specific functions (reusability again!). Thus a data dictionary can be used as a prime repository for the data entities and all attributes taking into account the requirements of all the proposed EDI transfers. There

should be no duplication of function at the lowest data item level.

One aspect that should not be missed is that if a data item is mandatory in a message it is mandatory in the subfunction and that subfunction is mandatory in the message.

The Activities

It should be possible to take the broad activities as documented in the first part of this modelling phase of message design, and build a picture of the activity requirements, possibly in a time based model. The BIM document referred to has the following to offer on a buying/selling activity. It is called a 'message sequence component of a scenario':

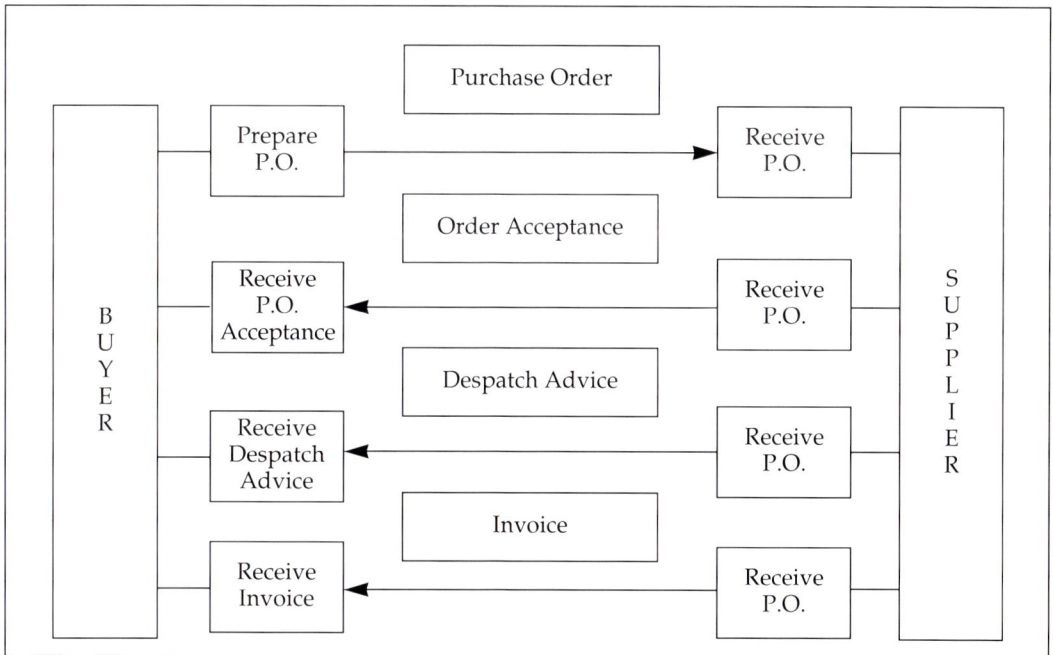

Figure 3: Message Sequence Component of a Scenario

Figure 3 showing supplier, buyer, their system activities and the transactions that take place between the two organisations, is self explanatory. Even though, as shown here, the activity model is simple, it should always be properly documented.

Electronic data interchange Message Development Guide

4.1.4 Message Design — This relates to boxes 5 and 6 of the BIM Framework at Table 3 The following has been taken from the UN/ECE BIM document and modified for the purposes of this document:

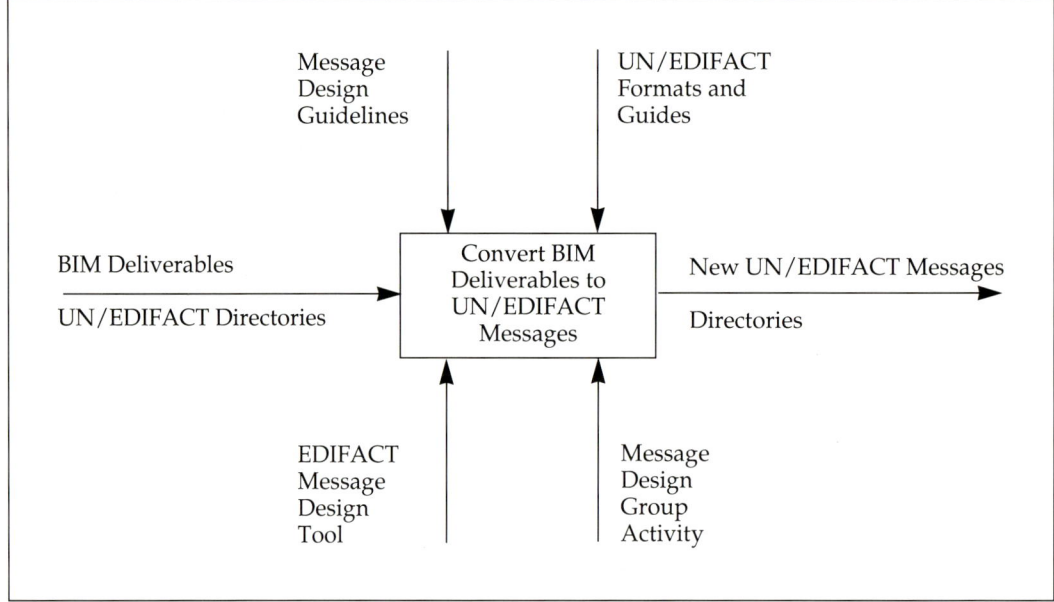

Figure 4: Message Design Inputs, Outputs, Controls and Resources

Inputs
It will be seen from Figure 4 that the inputs to the final message design phase are the:

- BIM deliverables

- UN/EDIFACT directories

- UN/EDIFACT message design guidelines

- UN/EDIFACT formats and guides

- Message design group activities.

BIM deliverables
These are the results of the activity and data modelling processes undertaken so far.

UN/EDIFACT directories
Never 're-invent the wheel'; certainly not where standards are concerned. A great deal of work and strife can be avoided by using the results of someone else's labours, provided they are appropriate, of course. It is vital to the message design process to obtain a set of UN/EDIFACT directories (see Chapter 4). This would normally be the latest set, however, there may be good reasons why an earlier set is appropriate. For example, if the move to EDI is being dictated by a customer or EDI partner or group that is using an earlier directory set than the latest one. Even in this case it is probably worthwhile obtaining the latest directories in order to see what, if any, changes have been made and/or data objects added.

UN/EDIFACT message design guidelines
The focus of this document and, in particular, this chapter, is on message design. The goal for the production of this document is that EDI message designers should, after studying it, be able to design messages without recourse to any other formal documentation other than the appropriate UN/EDIFACT directories. However, the EDI and EDIFACT world is changing fairly rapidly as new ideas are accepted and old conventions abandoned or changed. This document is based on the message design rules that are appropriate at the time of writing. It is known that, during 1996, changes are planned to the UN/EDIFACT message design guidelines. Depending upon the timing of the use of this document, therefore, it may be a good idea to get hold of the latest version of the UN/EDIFACT Message Design Guidelines. There is no doubt, however, that the further information provided in this document will still be appropriate on virtually every aspect.

UN/EDIFACT formats and guides
This input relates mainly to the understanding of how to lay out a message so that it is readable and understandable to all and particularly easy for someone

versed in UN/EDIFACT conventions. Furthermore, if for any reason message designers wish either to have their messages technically assessed for EDIFACT conformity, or wish to submit the messages into the EDIFACT process, then they should, naturally, follow the documentary conventions of UN/EDIFACT.

Also included in this input to message design is anything else that may be appropriate from the documents referred to in Chapter 3, eg the syntax rules and version/release conventions.

EDIFACT message design tools
EDIFACT message design tools are software packages that assist in the design of messages. For example, there are packages that hold directories of information, which can be updated, and which can be used to construct UN/EDIFACT messages. They work by taking data objects or groupings of data objects from the directories and building messages as instructed. In the more sophisticated of these packages comments and advice can be added.

The advantages of using a message design package are:

- enforcement of the rules

- the recording of requirements

- the reusability of elements

- the automation of maintenance

- the production and consistency in message design and documentation and user guides.

In 1995 there were not many of these packages on the market and some do not have all of the above qualities. There will, no doubt, be more forthcoming.

Message design group activities
Obviously, while designing messages, the input of the designing is important as decisions have to be made as to the best approach to take on different aspects. It should be pointed out here that EDIFACT message

design is not a precise art. There are a number of options that can be taken in designing messages each of which may work equally well. Nevertheless, there are certainly routes that should not be taken and these will be pointed out in this document. The objective, of course, is to get the information from one interchange partner to another unambiguously and as efficiently as possible. There are constraining factors to this, eg maintenance aspects, the context within which the message exists and other people's ideas.

Outputs
The outputs from the message design activity are:

- the messages themselves; and

- directories.

The messages
The messages which result from the modelling/design activity will, it is hoped, work and achieve the desired result. Of course, this is not the end of the activity. There is probably some optimisation to do as it is likely that, even though the messages may work, they will not be perfectly satisfactory immediately. Thus changes have to be agreed and message maintenance starts.

This is a good time to point out that, if the design work performed previously has not been documented properly, maintenance can be a headache. It is not always easy a year or more later to remember why something was done or why this option was chosen rather than the other. Thus, the prime output of this work is certainly the messages but they must be supplemented by good documentation of decisions made etc to get to where the message is now.

Directories
Although it could be argued that directories are simply one part of the good documentation, they have been mentioned separately because of their importance in maintaining a high quality maintenance process. It would be as well to structure the output directories in the same format as those issued by the UN/ECE. This standardisation makes them easy to understand and

Electronic data interchange Message Development Guide

helps to ensure that nothing has been omitted. An owner should be found who would be responsible for maintenance and distribution. That person would also be responsible for obtaining up-to-date EDIFACT directories and making comparisons with a view to stopping any divergence.

Any new design proposals should be channelled through the maintenance body. Thought should be given as to whether to disseminate documents to other government departments and agencies who are thought likely to be interested, and whether to submit the messages to the EDIFACT Board in order to achieve a more formal standardisation platform.

4.2   The foundation of UN/EDIFACT design – the syntax rules

The foundation of EDIFACT message design lies in the rules contained in ISO 9735. Although a thorough knowledge of all the rules contained in ISO 9735 is not necessary for message design, those rules that relate to how messages are constructed are relevant. Also, cognisance has to be taken of the way messages are identified in the message header segment as that segment, although normally described as a 'service segment', is usually included in the individual message documentation. It is from the data in the header segment (identified as UNH) that the software package that translates the message knows what it is translating. An EDIFACT message is simply a string of characters. This is shown in Figure 5 for a very small message.

UNH+PARTIN:D:93A:UN' BGM++1+2' DTM+7+1994122422359' FII+BK+123456 78:UNIVERSAL EXPORTPLC+:::010203:::BANK EXPORT+MOSKVA' RFF+VA T+123456789' DTM+7+19950101+102' NAD+MS+++UNIVERSAL EXPORT PLC +PO BOX 007:WHITEHALL+LONDON+WC1 0AA' CTA+AG+JAMES BOND' COM+01811112222:TE' UNS+D' NAD+AG+++UNIVERSAL EXPORT (RUSSIA)+PO BOX 57+MOSKVA' DTM+7+ 19951010+102' CTA+AG+IOSEF DZUGASHVILI' COM+1234-GO:TX' UNT+15+1'

Figure 5: Party Information (PARTIN) message

A message structure is based on logical groupings of data elements and those groups are nested hierarchically, as illustrated in Figure 6. Thus, single data elements are grouped into composite data elements (they are then called component data elements); single data elements and composite data elements are grouped into segments; segments are grouped into segment groups; and segments and segment groups are grouped into messages.

Chapter 4
How To Develop Messages

Furthermore, in order to show the full context of EDIFACT transmissions, it should be explained that messages can be grouped into functional groups or interchanges and functional groups of messages can be grouped into interchanges.

This is illustrated in ISO 9735 as follows:

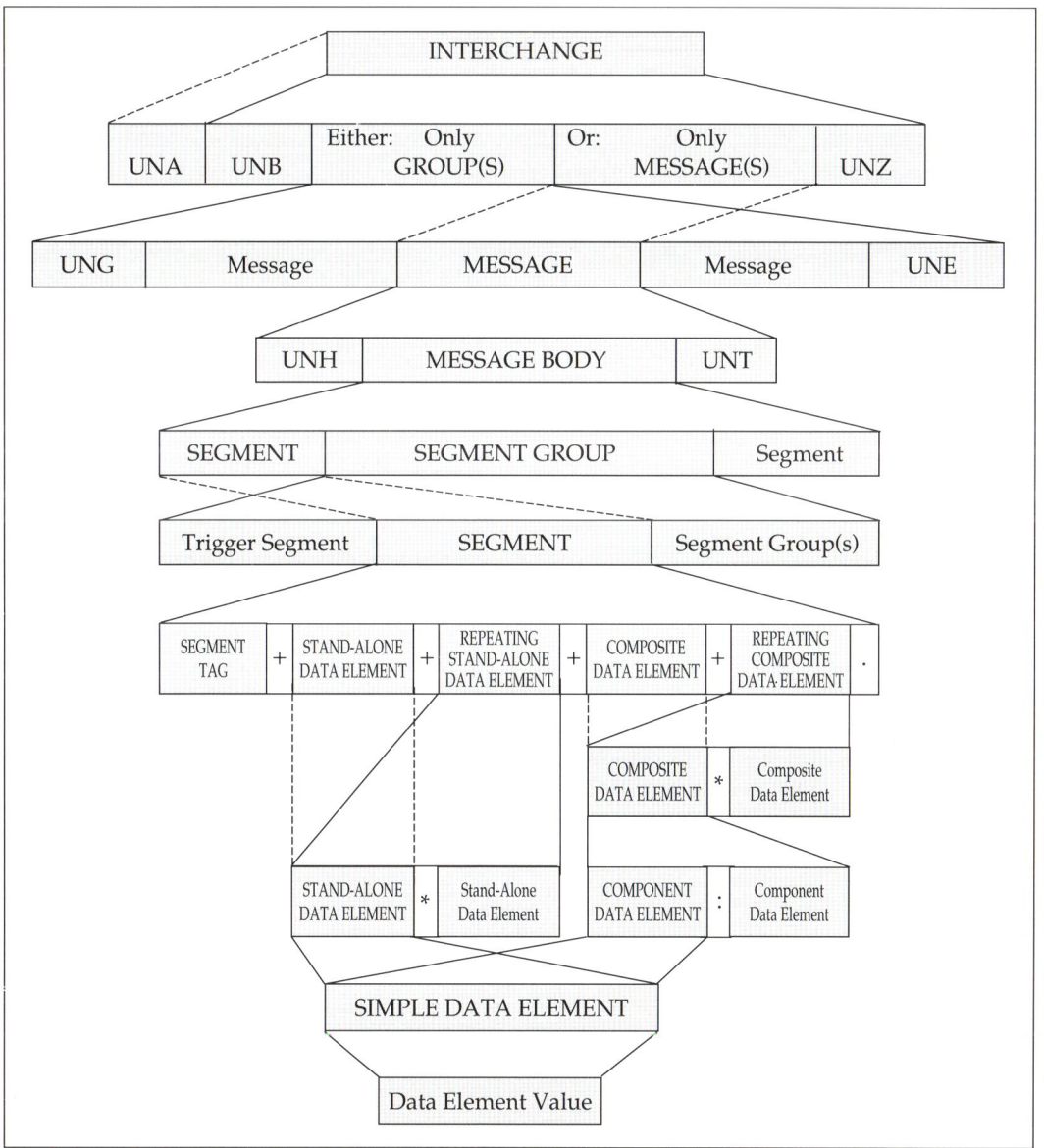

Figure 6: The Structure of EDIFACT

53

Electronic data interchange Message Development Guide

The use of repeating stand-alone data elements and repeating composite data elements is not part of version 3 of ISO 9735 but is expected to appear in version 4. Thus a breakdown into segments of the message shown in Figure 5 would be as follows:

```
UNH+1+PARTIN:D:93A:UN'
BGM++1+2'
DTM+7+1994122422359+202'
FII+BK+12345678:UNIVERSAL EXPORT PLC+:::010203:::BANK EXPORT+MOSKVA'
RFF+VAT+123456789'
DTM+7+19950101+102'
NAD+MS+++UNIVERSAL EXPORT PLC+PO BOX 007:WHITEHALL+LONDON+WC1 0AA'
CTA+AG+JAMES BOND'
COM+01811112222:TE'
UNS+D'
NAD+AG+++UNIVERSAL EXPORT (RUSSIA)+PO BOX 57+MOSKVA++SU'
DTM+7+19950101+102'
CTA+AG+IOSEF DZUGASHVILI'
COM+1234-GO:TX'
UNT+15+1'
```

Figure 7: Breakdown by segment of PARTIN message

It can be seen from Figure 7 that segments are identified by specific tags of three alphabetic characters (it is possible that figures may be used in the near future in special cases). These are the only structures, apart from the whole message, which are explicitly identified. All other structures are identified by their position in the message. That is to say, once an EDIFACT translation package identifies the start of the EDIFACT transmission, it knows what to expect as following. This, however, is not performed in the same way as a fixed format file that has to have blanks or nulls to indicate missing data. EDIFACT is more efficient than that. It uses special data separator characters that enable software packages to navigate through a message. Thus, the software is able to understand when an item of data is missing, be that item a data element, a composite data element, a segment or a segment group.

The separator characters mentioned above are, normally:

- a colon (:) to separate component data elements in a composite data element

- a plus sign (+) to separate stand alone data elements and composite data elements in a segment

- an apostrophe (') to denote the end of a segment.

It may be thought that using those characters would cause difficulty if they were required as part of the data, eg St Mary's Avenue as part of an address uses an apostrophe. However, a good software package will insert an escape character in the appropriate place to indicate what has happened. Alternatively, all or any of these characters can be changed if necessary to different ones. This is not recommended as a general practice, however.

A further point should be noted when considering efficiency in message design. For transmission, EDIFACT removes all non-significant zeros and non-significant spaces in data. This can be seen in the illustration of the EDIFACT message in Figure 5. They are restored by the translation software for the recipient's application.

One further aspect of message design that is based directly on the EDIFACT syntax rules is that data structures can be repeated up to a maximum stated number of times. This is explained further later.

4.3 Building a Message

So far this chapter has described the modelling activity that, ideally, should be undertaken to determine the data items to be sent in a particular message in order to fulfil its function, plus a brief introduction to the EDIFACT syntax rules that contain the basics of EDIFACT message design. This section describes the process of building a message using the data items resulting from the modelling activity, and applying the syntax rules and the rules taken from the UN/ECE's message design guidelines, plus general advice.

Electronic data interchange Message Development Guide

It is stated in Chapter 3 that the UN/ECE's message design guidelines are in the process of being updated. This process can be a long one (after all this is the world of standardisation!). However, it is not expected that the overall intent of the rules for message design themselves will change to any great extent. Any changes are likely to be in the form of a tightening up process, eg different semantics, the simplification of some rules and the removal of anomalies. This, paradoxically, will probably mean more rules, ie the complex rules broken down into simpler ones. Furthermore, there is likely to be a move towards greater recognition of the modelling process as described above.

This description of the message building process starts with the smallest units, ie data elements and continues with building these into logical structures and then combining those structures into larger ones and so on. However, one vitally important aspect that can save a great deal of time and trouble must not be forgotten at this stage. This is that there may be a message available to use already. Even if it does not fit exactly in terms of the data to be exchanged, consideration must be given to modifying the message or at least using it as a form of template. Thus, the UN/EDIFACT directories must be searched for such a message. **The UN/EDIFACT directories must be the starting point for all aspects of message design**. Thus, copies of the latest directories must be made available to the message designer.

Another point that should be borne in mind throughout the development of a message is that, as the work progresses towards the completed message, it is likely that some earlier processes/decisions will need to be revisited and possibly changes made. Message design is an iterative process. Do not forget to update, as necessary, documentation written earlier.

4.3.1 Data elements

It is assumed that there is no message already in existence that would suffice for the purpose intended. This means starting from scratch, that is, with a list of data items/objects which cannot be broken down into a lower level resulting from the modelling process, and which are required to be transmitted as a message. These need to be turned into data elements.

Chapter 4
How To Develop Messages

The data elements need to be named and given a short description of their usage. Also, each one will have a format (alpha, numeric etc) and a maximum length (3.3.4.1 above). Other attributes may be known. For example, if numeric, is there a need to consider the number of decimal places possible? Is the information that is represented by the data element essential for the message to make sense? These data elements should be listed with all the information that is known about them. No data element should duplicate the concept of another. Thus it may be necessary to make some compromises to align two or more objects with nearly similar descriptions.

The next step is to consult the UN/EDIFACT data element directory to see if some of the ideas are already covered by data elements in that directory. If they are, or can be by making insignificant changes to them, then a new list of data elements should be drawn up as the start of a serviceable local data element directory. For example, it may be that the data element in the UN/EDIFACT directory has a maximum length of 9 digits. However, if all that is needed are 6 digits then the UN data element will be perfectly adequate. The UN/EDIFACT data element tag should be used as the key for that data element in the local directory. If the UN/EDIFACT data element length is 6 characters and 9 are required, then that poses a problem, the answer to which depends upon the extent of the requirement to align precisely with UN/EDIFACT. A tag that is placed in the series x7xx to x9xx (3.4 above) should be used with a note against the data element cross referring it to the UN/EDIFACT data element and describing the difference(s). As regards the tag, it should be noted that a data element that requires a code for its value should have an odd-numbered tag. Others should be even numbered.

If a pair of data elements are required to express a concept, one in coded form and one in clear text, then the numbers shall be consecutive, with the coded number the higher of the two (see the example of a composite data element below). Also, coded data elements are almost exclusively defined as variable length maximum 3 alphanumeric characters. These may sound petty rules,

Electronic data interchange Message Development Guide

but they do make for a well-organised directory.
A data element can be used on its own in a segment (stand alone) and in a composite data element.

4.3.2 Composite Data Elements

It is certain that, as a result of the modelling process, concepts will emerge that can only be satisfied by using more than one data element, ie two or more as a logical group. This should result in the formation of a composite data element (or segment – see below). The first rule in defining a composite data element is to use one from the UN/EDIFACT directory if it exists. If there is one in the directory that nearly covers the concept required, a decision has to be made as to whether it can be used, or what the ramifications are in using it slightly amended (in which case the UN/EDIFACT tag cannot be used).

An example of a composite is:

C076 COMMUNICATION CONTACT
Desc: Communication number of a department or employee in a specified channel.
010 3148   Communication number   M an..25
020 3155   Communication channel qualifier M an..3

This composite is to enable the transmission of telephone, fax etc numbers. The number would go in data element 3148 and the appropriate code for the mode (eg fax, E-mail) would be taken from the code list associated with data element 3155. 3155 is a qualifier data element and the role of this type of data element and the rules that apply to its use are explained in 4.3.3 below.

It will be noted that the composite has an identifier (C076). This is its key in the directory file. The C stands for composite – the other composites are service segment composites which start with S and interactive EDI composites which start with an E. The number is simply sequential. The first set of numbers in the above example – 010 to 020 – are sequential within the composite, and allow for the insertion of new data elements between the component data elements (a rare event, as it is better to add to the end for processing compatibility purposes). Both data elements are mandatory (M) if the composite is used.

There is no rule stating the maximum number of component data elements that can be in a composite data element. In UN/EDIFACT there are composites with ten components. Beyond that number the message designer should be thinking of, perhaps, splitting the composite into smaller units and using two or more composites. The viability of this would depend on the concept(s) being considered.

There is a need to consider whether more than one occurrence of a data element is needed in a composite. The following is an example of a UN/EDIFACT composite where there is an obvious reason for repetition, as a range normally needs two numbers.

```
C208  IDENTITY NUMBER RANGE
7402  Identity number              M  an..35
7402  Identity number              C  an..35
```

There is a special way of identifying certain codes in composite data elements. Obviously codes are preferred to text in EDI because codes make computer processing more efficient. The code lists containing the values that are sent in coded data elements are very extensive in UN/EDIFACT and are published as part of the directory sets. However, UN/EDIFACT code lists are not all embracing.

Other organisations maintain code lists, eg the ISO country code list, and, therefore, it is necessary for UN/EDIFACT to make provision for the use of codes from these lists. This is achieved by the use of a pair of data elements, one identifying the owner of the code list and the other the list itself (an outside owner may maintain more than one list). In the example below, the owner is identified in data element 3055 and the particular code list in data element 1131.

```
C002  DOCUMENT/MESSAGE NAME
Desc: Identification of a type of document/message by
code or name. Code preferred.
010  1001  Document/message name, coded    C an..3
020  1131  Code list qualifier              C an..3
030  3055  Code list responsible agency, coded  C an..3
040  1000  Document/message name            C an..35
```

It will be noted that all the data elements in this composite are conditional. However, if the composite is used at least one must be present and this, obviously, must include 1001 or 1000 (preferably 1001). It may be considered that in a particular application there is no need for all these data elements and that the requirement can be satisfied by using only data element 1001. If this is the case, and due thought must be given to the future before making a decision, then that data element could be used as a stand-alone data element in a segment.

It is a matter of best practice in designing composite data elements to place all mandatory data elements before conditional data elements and the most used conditional data elements before the least used. This is for efficiency in transmission. For example, in a fictitious transmission using all the data elements in the composite the transmission looks like:

......other data ......+17:147:1:combined cert. of value/origin+.......other data......

where   17 = the code for a combined certificate of value and origin
147 = documents requested by Customs
1 = the Customs Co-operation Council

combined cert. of value/origin = the plain text description of code 17. (More information would be likely to be in the code list.)

If the code and text only were sent, the transmission would look like this:
.......other data ......+17::combined cert. of value/origin+....other data......

If the text alone was sent, the transmission would look like this:
.......other data......+:::combined cert. of value/origin....other data.....

If the code alone was sent, the transmission would look like this:
.......other data......+17+.....other data.......

So there is a saving according to whether codes are sent instead of text, and in separator characters depending upon the order of the data in the composite.

It must be emphasised that the above example has been concocted purely for this illustration – there is probably no Customs Co-operation Council code list of this nature.

4.3.3 Segments

Segments are logical groupings of data elements in much the same way as composite data elements, although segments can include composite data elements as well as stand-alone (simple single) data elements.

When looking for the logical groupings of objects, as required by the modelling activity, it is as well to look at both the UN/EDIFACT composite data element directory and the segment directory for the required combination. There are, currently, no stated rules as to when a segment should be created as opposed to a composite data element, the decision is more difficult to make when there are only a few data elements to consider making into a group. The more data elements there are the more there is a tendency to make a segment. However, it depends upon the concept being created. For example, a structure for date and time (see below) is a composite on its own in a segment.

There are a large number of concepts that are used in many messages, eg name, address, date/time and references. There are UN/EDIFACT structures already defined for these and they should be used where required. The UN/EDIFACT segment for date/time/period is structured as follows:

```
DTM      DATE/TIME/PERIOD
Function: to specify date, and/or time, or period
010   C507 DATE/TIME/PERIOD                   M
      2005 Date/time/period qualifier         M  an..3
      2380 Date/time/period                   C  an..35
      2379 Date/time/period format qualifier  C  an..3
```

Note that the segment identifier is DTM that is sent in transmission. Data element 2005 contains a code indicating the context of the date or time or period, eg delivery (date), invoice (date); 2380 is for the actual date or time or period and, because it is based on the ISO standard for dates and times, 2379 indicates the format of 2380, eg YYMMDD. Even though it looks as though the composite C507 could be used in other segments, this is not so. Where one composite makes up the segment, and that concept is required in a message, the segment is used.

The following is another example of a UN/EDIFACT segment for which the intent is to provide details of pricing in the appropriate message. It is a useful segment to use for illustrative purposes as it contains several UN/EDIFACT concepts.

Note that segment names, composite names and stand-alone data element names are written in upper case while component data element names are written in lower case. This is a UN/EDIFACT convention that is quite useful. It makes a message or segment easier to read and, therefore, less likely to be misunderstood.

PRI   PRICE DETAILS
Function: To specify price information.
010   C509 PRICE INFORMATION   C
      5125 Price qualifier   M an..3
      5118 Price   C n..15
      5375 Price type, coded   C an..3
      5387 Price type qualifier   C an..3
      5284 Unit price basis   C n..9
      6411 Measure unit qualifier   C an..3
020   5213 SUB-LINE PRICE CHANGE, CODED C an..3

Data Element Types (qualifiers etc)
Data elements can be categorised into three basic types (there are other flavours) – qualified data elements, non-qualified data elements and qualifiers.

A qualified data element is one that needs further detail to make it useful. If the PRI segment above is to be useful in a number of different concepts, data element 5118, price, needs to be qualified in order to indicate to what sort of price it relates. For example, it could be contract price, catalogue price or discounted price. In order to do this a qualifier data element has to be associated with it.

Chapter 4
How To Develop Messages

Thus in the PRI segment, 5118 Price is followed by 5375 Price type coded. The code in the latter data element qualifies the value in the former. A qualifier code is always defined as alphanumeric, maximum length 3 characters (an..3).

The rule is that when a single data element has to be qualified, the qualifier always follows that data element in the composite. Note that it has to be a composite because the two data elements have to be treated as a pair.

5213 Sub-line price change, coded is a non-qualified data element.

When creating data elements it is as well to try to make them generic, if possible. This has been the UN/EDIFACT approach and it means easier maintenance of the data element directory although, because of this policy, the code lists get rather long. It was stated above that a qualifier data element always follows the data element it qualifies and yet in the PRI segment, a qualifier is the first data element. This is because 5125 Price qualifier qualifies the whole composite C509. This is again an EDIFACT rule in message construction, ie if the composite has to be qualified then that qualifier has to be the first data element. This rule also applies to segments.

As with composites, for reasons of efficiency, mandatory stand-alone and mandatory composite data elements should always be placed at the beginning of a segment. Of the remaining conditional data elements and composites the most used (if this can be determined) should precede the least used. This rule has less precedence that the ones about the position of qualifiers, ie at the beginning of the structures they qualify, although it will be noted that most segment and composite qualifiers in UN/EDIFACT messages are designated as mandatory anyway – probably to override the anomaly.

Repetition
When designing a message it may be found necessary to repeat logical groups of data. Below is an example of a

segment containing repeating data elements within repeating composites. In this case repeating data element 7402 would allow a set of numbers to be transmitted. Repeating data element 7402 in composite C208 allows, also, a range of numbers to be transmitted. The type of number is indicated by a code in data element 7405.

GIN   GOODS IDENTITY NUMBER
Function: To give specific identification numbers, either as single numbers or ranges.
```
010   7405  IDENTITY NUMBER QUALIFIER    M  an..3
020   C208  IDENTITY NUMBER RANGE        M
      7402  Identity number              M  an..35
      7402  Identity number              C  an..35
030   C208  IDENTITY NUMBER RANGE        C
      7402  Identity number              M  an..35
      7402  Identity number              C  an..35
040   C208  IDENTITY NUMBER RANGE        C
      7402  Identity number              M  an..35
      7402  Identity number              C  an..35
050   C208  IDENTITY NUMBER RANGE        C
      7402  Identity number              M  an..35
      7402  Identity number              C  an..35
060   C208  IDENTITY NUMBER RANGE        C
      7402  Identity number              M  an..35
      7402  Identity number              C  an..35
```

Having looked at the structures of both composite data elements and segments, it will be apparent that there is a fairly wide choice for the message designer to choose one or the other for a logical group of data elements. As there are no rules, precedence (from the latest directories) is the best method of gaining guidance as to the choice.

It is recommended that the latest UN/ECE directories are studied in order to get a feeling for the conventions used and to see if there are any parallels that can help. The number of data elements, the function (broad or narrow) and the context of use (generic, specific) are all factors that can come into play. Whatever the choice, it should work. However, do not forget the usage of any structure in the future – in new messages and for easy maintenance.

Segment Tags
The last task of the message designer in respect to creating segments is to provide them with a tag. Obviously, the tag should not be identical to that in any other directory for a different segment. Avoid tags starting with a 'U' as these are reserved for the syntactical service segments. It often helps the designer and reader of the message, although it makes no difference to the software, to create tags with meaningful letters (eg FII – Financial Institution Information). This does not necessarily help with translation into other languages.

4.3.4 Segment Groups

Segment groups are not very well described in ISO 9735 (the EDIFACT syntax). In fact they appear only as examples. Therefore, the UN/ECE's Message Design Guidelines and the UN/ECE message directories have to be consulted for the usage of segment groups in UN/EDIFACT messages. The omission of segment grouping from the syntax rules document is likely to be corrected in the next issue.

It is important to note that segment groups do not have specific identifiers or tags and there is no UN/EDIFACT directory of them. However, there are particular groups of segments that are used in a number of different messages for the same purpose. Therefore, it is wise to pick these for use, if appropriate.

Once the message designer has decided on the full set of segments required for a particular message, the next step is to determine if there is a need to group those segments into higher level groups. The modelling process may have determined which segments go together as a set in terms of their function. For example, if there is a requirement for organisation names and addresses to be transmitted as part of the data, there may also be a requirement to send relevant contact names and their telephone and fax numbers. Also, there may be some relevant banking details required for those particular organisations.

Electronic data interchange Message Development Guide

The following is a set of segments, which it can be seen form a logical group, and which were taken from the UN/EDIFACT messages directories to illustrate this function.

NAD   NAME AND ADDRESS
Function: To specify the name/address and their related function, either by C082 only and/or unstructured by C058 or structured by C080 through 3207.

```
010  3035  PARTY QUALIFIER                          M an..3
020  C082  PARTY IDENTIFICATION
             DETAILS                                C
      3039  Party id. Identification                M an..35
      1131  Code list qualifier                     C an..3
      3055  Code list responsible agency, coded     C an..3
030  C058  NAME AND ADDRESS                         C
      3124  Name and address line                   M an..35
      3124  Name and address line                   C an..35
      3124  Name and address line                   C an..35
      3124  Name and address line                   C an..35
      3124  Name and address line                   C an..35
040  C080  PARTY NAME                               C
      3036  Party name                              M an..35
      3036  Party name                              C an..35
      3036  Party name                              C an..35
      3036  Party name                              C an..35
      3036  Party name                              C an..35
      3045  Party name format, coded                C an..3
050  C059  STREET                                   C
      3042  Street and number/PO. box               M an..35
      3042  Street and number/PO. box               C an..35
      3042  Street and number/PO. box               C an..35
060  3164  CITY NAME                                C an..35
070  3229  COUNTRY SUB-ENTITY
             IDENTIFICATION                         C an..9
080  3251  POSTCODE IDENTIFICATION                  C an..9
090  3207  COUNTRY, CODED                           C an..3
```

CTA   CONTACT INFORMATION
Function: To identify a person or a department to whom communication should be directed.

```
010  3139  CONTACT FUNCTION, CODED                  C an..3
     020  C056  DEPARTMENT OR EMPLOYEE
                  DETAILS                           C
           3413  Department or employee
                   identification                   C an..17
```

```
           3412  Department or employee      C an..35
COM   COMMUNICATION CONTACT
```
Function: To identify a communication number of a department or a person to whom communication should be directed.
```
010  C076  COMMUNICATION CONTACT            M
      3148  Communication number            M an..25
      3155  Communication channel
            qualifier                       M an..3
```
As can be seen the segments are NAD, CTA and COM. If one each of these was included in a message structure then the only possibility would be to send one organisation name, one contact and one communication number (phone or fax). The transmission would be :

.......other segments.....NAD CTA COM.........other segments.......

In most cases this is not enough. More than one address is required, with more than one contact and each contact having more than one communications channel. If this requirement was satisfied by repeating each segment as many times as necessary the following may be transmitted:

.......other segments.....NAD NAD CTA CTA CTA COM COM.........other segments.......

However, with this transmission it is not possible to know which communications channel belongs to which contact who belongs to which organisation. To allow proper linkages to be formed the segments have to be structured into a hierarchical group. This is pictorially illustrated as follows:

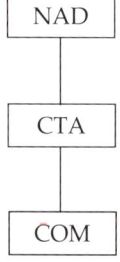

Figure 8: Combination of NAD, CTA and COM segments

Electronic data interchange Message Development Guide

where each repeat of an NAD segment is followed by a CTA segment then a COM segment. Another way of stating it is that the segments are nested, the one below within the one above. If there were more than one NAD, the loop would be passed through again. The maximum number of repetitions for each segment has to be stated as has its status (mandatory or conditional). The status symbol (M or C) is sometimes called the requirement designator – especially in the USA.

The message designer has, therefore, to indicate status and number of repeats of each segment. This could be written as follows:

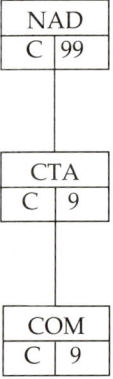

Figure 9: Combination of NAD, CTA and COM segments with repeats (1)

Another combination of these three segments is:

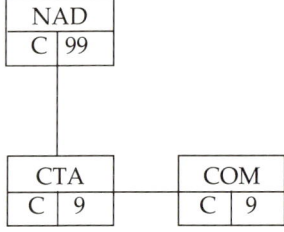

Figure 10: Combination of NAD, CTA and COM segments with repeats (2)

As the processing in this instance would be up to ninety-nine NAD's, followed by up to nine CTA segments, followed by up to nine COM segments, there would still be a problem knowing which of the COM's related to which of the CTA's. There may not be an equivalent number as the above structure allows, for example, up to nine CTA's and up to nine COM's including zero in each structure independently. So in a particular circumstance there may be three CTA segments and five COM's, or only one COM. If there was ever going to be only one CTA then there would be no problem in this structure.

The circumstance where the message designer has to cater for more than one name and address and closely associated data cannot be ignored or left ambiguous. The answer is achieved by identifying a repeating group that is indicated in documentation as follows:

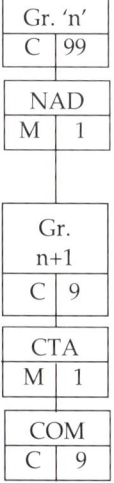

Figure 11: Segment grouping (a)

or, where there is no need to constrain a many to many relationship (ie there is, in this instance, only one CTA necessary) where 'n' is the sequential number of the group in the message. This group number is just a document format convention and the number does not appear in the message when transmitted.

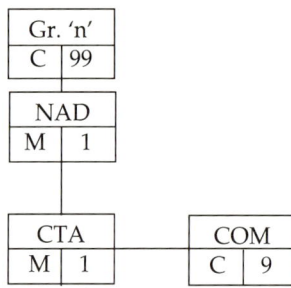

Figure 12: Segment grouping (b)

The above documentary layouts of parts of message structures are called branching diagrams. There is a rival format called a segment table. Figure 11 and Figure 12 above would be shown as:

```
────── Segment Group 'n' ──────    C 99 ┐
NAD  Name and address              M 1  │
────── Segment Group 'n+1' ────    C 9 ┐│
CTA  Contact information           M 1 ││
COM  Communication contact         C 9
```

Table 4: Segment table equivalent of Figure 11

```
────── Segment Group 'n' ──────    C 99 ┐
NAD  Name and address              M 1  │
CTA  Contact information           C 1  │
COM  Communication contact         C 9  ┘
```

Table 5: Segment table equivalent of Figure 12

In UN/EDIFACT repetitions are shown as 1, 9, 99, 999 etc. This is only a convention.

To reiterate, remembering that EDIFACT messages are read top to bottom then left to right:

In Table 4:

- segment group 'n' can repeat up to 99 times and because it is conditional it may be omitted from the message transmission (if there is no data for it in any particular instance)

- segment NAD is mandatory and, therefore, none of the other segments can carry data without an NAD being present. This is called the trigger segment for the group and in designing a message the trigger segment shall always be mandatory and occur (repeat) once. If more are needed the whole segment group is repeated.

- segment Group n+1 is conditional. It, therefore, can be omitted from a transmission if there is no data for CTA and for COM. Otherwise, it can occur up to 9 times

- CTA can only appear once in any CTA/COM loop

- COM cannot appear without a CTA.

In Table 5;

- the first two bullets of (a) apply, but

- CTA is conditional, therefore, it need not appear at all in any transmission of the group. If there were up to nine repeats of the CTA segment they would all appear in sequence after each loop starting with NAD

- all occurrences of COM in each loop, triggered by NAD, would be together. If there was no CTA data, COM data could follow NAD data.

4.3.5 The Message

The message designer will now have, after applying the guidance above, a set of segment groups and segments that have not been made part of a group. These have to be ordered into a complete message structure. Some message structures will be quite complex, others small and easy to understand. The complex ones can cause problems of comprehension and possible ambiguity. The important factor, therefore, is to keep everything as simple as possible.

It is possible that simplicity is more important than efficiency, as the maintenance costs will be higher when amending a complex message structure, particularly if the task is given to someone who did not design the original message. The following illustrates what a fairly simple documented message may look like.

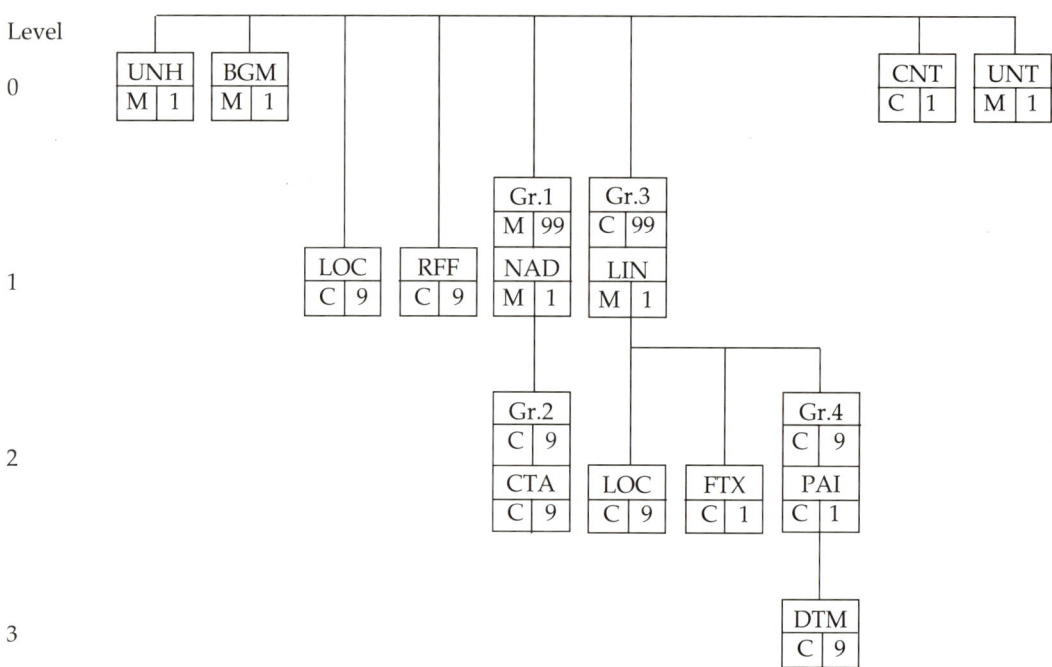

Figure 13: A Message Branching Diagram

It makes it easier to appreciate if the segments in Figure 13 are explained.

UNH – the Message Header that contains the identity of the message.

BGM – Beginning of Message segment contains general information about the message Most UN/EDIFACT messages have a mandatory BGM, but it is not compulsory.

LOC – Locations (places) general

RFF – References

NAD – Names and addresses

CTA – Contact names

LIN – Line items

LOC – Locations relative to line items

FTX – Free text relative to line items

PAI – Payment instructions relative to line items

DTM – Dates/times/periods relative to payment instructions

CNT – Count

UNT – The message trailer

It should be noted that there is no theoretical limit to the number of times a segment can be used in a message. Thus, in some long messages a segment that is there to contain, say, 'references', will appear in several places. It will be, in a sense, qualified by the group it is in or its place in the message. For example, there may be some references connected to a name and address. More likely there will be references related to banking information or transport details. Where banking information is structured as a segment group, and similarly with transport details, the RFF (UN/EDIFACT) reference segment will appear in both groups.

Collisions

The occurrence of the same segment type in different places in a message can cause the message designer some problems. For example, in the above message, there are two LOC segments. One relates to the whole message, but would be overridden by data in the second LOC in respect of line items, eg a general delivery location for all merchandise, except for specific instructions in the second LOC segment for a particular goods line item.

If the first LOC segment was placed between segment group 4 and CNT and, in a particular transmission, if there was no data for group 4, then there would be one LOC segment immediately following another. If both carried data then it would be impossible to tell when the first LOC repeats had finished and the second started (each can have up to nine). This problem is called a collision. A collision can be avoided by:

1. Moving the segments and/or groups around so that there is a mandatory segment or mandatory segment group, at the same level, in between the two problem segments.

2. Inserting a mandatory UNS segment in the appropriate place.

As far as 1 above is concerned, the idea is fairly self explanatory. However, collisions are sometimes difficult to spot (look particularly closely at trigger segments). One method of segment placement that lessens the chance of collisions is to place, at the same level (Fig 12), all free standing segments before segment groups.

In respect to 2 above, there is a segment in UN/EDIFACT that has the specific function of separating distinct parts of a message. This is the UNS Section Control segment. Many potential collision situations occur because message designers, quite legitimately, divide their messages into header, detail and trailer sections. This is explained in more detail below. However, to help in avoiding collisions, the UNS segment would have to be mandatory.

There has been some discussion in UN/EDIFACT message design circles about the use of UNS and the feeling has been that it should not be used specifically to avoid collisions. The latest moves, however, have a more relaxed mood and it may be that message designers will be given a freer hand to use collision avoidance segments.

A further possibility as regards collision avoidance that some industries are adopting is the use of specific trigger segments. For example, if a convention was adopted in a message design that each or some trigger segments were tagged in the series Snn, where nn is a sequential number, then potential collisions can be avoided. A segment such as this cannot, however, be designed without data elements and, currently, data must be sent in it.

There are moves, however, to amend the syntax to allow 'empty' segments to be transmitted in the form AAA' (Segment tag immediately followed by segment terminator.) Because the tag is not transmitted when there is no data for a conditional segment, these segments would have to have a mandatory status.

Message Sections
Many messages are designed to be the equivalent of forms. Many forms have header, detail and summary information. For example, in an invoice, for header information there could be data relating to the original purchase order, the delivered address and references all relating to the whole invoice. This could be followed by details of goods sent with individual prices and specific changes to the header information for individual goods items etc. Finally, could appear summary information containing, among other things, VAT and other control totals.

Although it is not necessary for software to base its processing on the technique, from a human legibility point of view a message with sections is often easier to read and understand. If the data in the detail is supposed to override that in header segments, it presupposes there are equivalent segments there – poised for collision (see above)!

As stated above, there is a specific service segment that performs the task of separating sections of a message. It is always used at level zero in a message structure and contains either a 'D' indicating that detail follows, or 'S' indicating that summary information follows. It is not necessary always to use both in a message. Details of the UNS segment do not appear in the UN/EDIFACT message etc. directories but in the syntax (ISO 9735) which describes it as follows:

Segment: UNS, Section Control

Function: To separate Header, Detail and Summary sections of a message

NOTE: To be used by message designers when required to avoid ambiguities.
Mandatory only if specified for the type of message concerned.

Ref.	Repr.		Name	Remarks
0081	a1	M	SECTION IDENTIFICATION	Separates sections in a message by one of the following codes:
				D separates the header and detail sections
				S separates the detail and summary sections

Table 6: UNS Section Control

It should be noted that there is a proposal, which is likely to succeed, to change the representation from a1 to an1 and to allow more codes than D and S to be used.

Message Identification
Once a message has been completed, the message has to be tagged and named. The convention is a six alphabetic tag that is reasonably meaningful, eg INVOIC for

invoice, ORDERS for purchase order and, PAYORD for payment order. It should go without saying that every effort should be made not to use tags and names already in use.

4.4 Message Implementation Guides

In the early days of message design in UN/EDIFACT the goal was to define structures that could be used, as defined, across industry and internationally. This proved a difficult goal because, with the introduction of different industry and national requirements, many data elements were included which were redundant to any particular industry. Furthermore, new users who had little knowledge of the original message building process, needed more information to make the message easily to implement. Thus, industries in particular, began to define sub-sets of the messages (in some cases cutting down the size of the message by more than one half) and adding information (allowable codes etc) to assist implementation for their own usage. Unfortunately this provided an opportunity for divergence.

In terms of the 'trade' messages (invoice, purchase order etc) in the UK, this problem was realised and implementation guides constructed, with the participation of the industries concerned, where the core information used in all the sub-sets was the same. These messages are published by the UK's Article Number Association (ANA) under the title 'UK EDIFACT Trade Message Convention'. It is a useful guide on how to structure implementation guides.

For the designer of proprietary messages in government, much of the information required for implementation will have been uncovered in the design stage – and documented. This will make it easier to fill the implementation guide with the required information. It is unlikely that with proprietary messages that sub-sets will need to be defined but, if they are, the rules for sub-setting as set out in Chapter 3 must be followed.

4.5 Maintenance

The importance of thinking about message maintenance has been mentioned earlier in the Chapter. In general terms, in the IT industry, maintenance of applications can be significantly costly. When developing messages, therefore, it is necessary to think ahead as to what the effect of any decision will be on maintenance activities. Keeping things simple cannot be emphasised too strongly. When the message developers move on to other work, it would be very unfortunate for their organisations for them to have left behind a legacy of complex and badly documented message structures/implementation guides.

Do not have a blinkered outlook and design messages purely for the moment. Goals should have been determined in the early message design stage that most likely included widening the use of EDI to other areas. This may mean that the current message design has to be changed slightly. Any changes should be predetermined and controlled.

Times change. It will be worthwhile, in the maintenance stage to keep an eye on what is happening in other related areas, particularly in the sphere of message standards. This may mean keeping up to date with the UN/EDIFACT directories. Watch out for new software developments. What are designers of new applications building at the front end of their applications for EDI? How will this affect the designed messages? Check for new tools being developed to assist in message maintenance.

A message is not often developed in a vacuum. There is normally the proposed sender and receiver involved. Keep in touch regularly with the other party or parties. At least this will avoid unwelcome surprises and could generate efficiencies.

Regarding specific advice regarding the amendment of 'live' messages, it does no harm to revert to the general rules for message development. Specifically, add new data elements to the end of composites and segments (unless they are mandatory) and be aware of changes in structure that could potentially allow collisions to occur.

4.6 Multi-format Objects

EDIFACT is an EDI messaging standard for sending formatted strings of characters taken from, generally, a trading or administrative application. There are other applications where data is required to be transmitted from one computer system to another, where EDIFACT is not the appropriate standard. For example, there are standards such as IGES and STEP for the formatting of drawings etc. Very often there is a need to send not only the drawings, X-rays or other kinds of pictures (often generically referred to as binary data), but also data about them. The appropriate standard for this explanatory data may be EDIFACT.

Work is being undertaken in the UN/EDIFACT world to define, generally two approaches. Firstly, there is the embedding of 'binary' data into EDIFACT structures. It is unlikely that a structure will be defined which will allow 'binary' data to be embedded into messages (although it is possible and is done in the ANSI X12 standard – see later). More than likely a structure that can contain a 'binary object' will be defined which is at the equivalent level to an EDIFACT message in the EDIFACT Interchange. Secondly, it has to be recognised that related EDIFACT data and 'binary objects', may not emanate from the same system or be sent, conveniently at the same time.

In both of the instances outlined above, there is a need to define a way of relating the different kinds of data. A standard means of cross referencing is being developed and should be available for testing in 1996. This, where necessary, needs to be considered in designing messages.

4.7 Interactive EDI (I-EDI)

The first international EDI standards to be developed were for what are now beginning to be called 'batch' messages. These are single transmissions of data, mostly through a value added networks, where time, in terms of minutes, is not the prime factor. They are often large blocks of data that are processed serially by sending and receiving applications.

Other applications do not work in this way. They require a more conversational approach, often driven by a human at a VDU. The prime example of this is the travel agent booking a flight and/or a hotel etc by getting into various systems. The reasons for using standardised EDI messages in these applications are the same as those for 'batch' EDI but the EDI transmissions take the form of queries and responses to those queries.

Available now from the UN/ECE is a draft syntax for I-EDI. Messages are being developed in the travel, tourism and leisure industry for use by airlines, tour operators, etc. These are in their early stages, but pilot testing is going on and a draft interactive directory of data elements etc is available. HM Customs and Excise have been using I-EDI for some time now for Customs clearance of goods at ports. Another UK application is the UNICORN project for, largely, cross channel ferry booking. There are likely to be more and more applications that could benefit from an interactive approach as the techniques become better defined.

I-EDI messaging in UN/EDIFACT format is in its infancy. Currently most messages are being defined in very much the same way as for batch EDI apart from the following differences:

- There is a greater use of specific data elements, rather than the generic ones plus qualifiers that has been the approach for batch EDI. This makes for more efficient transfers, when one data element can be sent rather than two. Spread this over a whole message and the saving can be considerable. This has meant creating an I-EDI directory of data elements etc.

- slightly different approach is being taken to qualifying whole messages where particular industry requirements are identified by a code in the Message Header segment.

A further difference that is thought likely to emerge is that messages will be defined as small sub-structures that, when the data from several are added together, satisfy a complete business transaction.

In respect to government message design, I-EDI should present an interesting opportunity. The same processes of modelling and message design should be undertaken as for the batch messages but with the latest I-EDI directories. It is also important to obtain a copy of the latest syntax rules, as these differ from the batch ones in certain instances, but in the main, to see how messages are controlled between dialogue initiator and responder. This will provide the context in which the messages are transferred and which will assist in message development.

4.8 Other Standards

There are two other base EDI messaging standards which the UK Government may come across and which, therefore, are worthwhile explaining. The two are:

- UN/GTDI or TRADACOMS, and

- ANSI X12.

UN/GTDI (United Nations Guidelines for Trade Data Interchange) is also sometimes referred to as UN/TDI. In practice, there is a slight difference to the syntax rules in each but not the message structures. Whether the reference is to one or the other, it should not matter for the purposes of this document. TRADACOMS (Trade Data Communications) has been coupled with UN/GTDI because they are essentially the same, also. The TRADACOMS standards, which are the responsibility of the UK's Article Number Association, have been implemented by more users than any other standard for EDI in the UK. EDIFACT is, however, catching up and is the international standard and recommended for government use.

Some work has been done in the TRADACOMS area to define EDIFACT messages that have in them all the functionality of the particular TRADACOMS messages. These are in the UK/EDIFACT Trade Message Convention documentation supplied by the ANA. ANSI X12 (American National Standards Institute, X12 Committee) is used widely in the USA and in some other developed countries. There is little use of it in the UK, and it is unlikely that the UK Government will meet it much – only those departments with links to US Government departments and the armed forces.

The parents of EDIFACT were, in fact, UN/TDI and ANSI X12. Thus, there are common structures, overall. However, this does not mean that UN/TDI or ANSI X12 messages can be directly transposed into EDIFACT messages or vice versa. The problem is at data element level. There are few exact equivalents and the semantics are different. The easiest process is to translate from one standard to a flat file and then translate that file into the other standard. Even so the data element equivalents still have to be worked out and data manipulation problems abound.

If there is a need for both partners in an EDI partnership to migrate from other standards to EDIFACT, then the full process of proper modelling and design will probably reap benefits – by allowing some short cuts to be taken. The aim for long-term efficiency and robustness need to be borne in mind as significantly important.

5 Security And Legal Issues

This chapter covers the reasons for requiring security on EDI messages and ways in which to counter threats. There is also a short discussion on the legal issues surrounding EDI transfers.

5.1 Security

Security for EDI is not a special case; whenever financial or sensitive information passes between two parties, steps are taken to ensure that the information moves securely between the two.

Because EDI messages tend to be commercial or administrative in nature, normal rules of security apply to them. Security needs to address the following threats:

- Repudiation; sender or recipient denying the transaction has taken place. For instance, a sender having ordered goods might claim never to have sent the order to avoid cancellation charges

- Masquerading, also referred to as spoofing or aliasing; third party pretending to be legitimate trading partner

- Interception and modification; any party recording, replaying, re-routing, modifying or deleting a valid message

- Fraud; illegal misuse of a message for monetary gain.

Not all EDI security techniques are covered here, as it is a new field and many techniques will become of more or less importance as time passes. Aspects and techniques that are in common use or which appear to be heading towards becoming standard are covered below.

Note that the term 'encryption' is used here to mean converting plain text to ciphered text to protect its confidentiality, whereas the term cryptography is more generic and can apply to digital signatures.

5.1.1 Threats

5.1.1.1 Interception

Interception of an EDI data stream allows third parties to monitor and/or modify the data. Modification is covered in 5.1.1.4, so means of securing confidentiality are discussed here.

In the non-EDI world confidentiality is ensured by physically protecting a document – by putting it in an envelope, sending it by courier, etc. For EDI, confidentiality can be maintained in several ways:

- Use a closed private network. This does not ensure confidentiality within the network provider's organisation

- Use encryption to prevent disclosure of sensitive information following unauthorised interception of an EDI message. The quality and strength of the encryption needs to be carefully considered when setting up electronic communications between trading partners. In government, advice should be sought from the security authorities

- Combination of above. Limits the number of possible attempts at reading data while giving some protection against all but the most dedicated infiltrator.

The usual way of encrypting an EDI message is to use symmetric cryptography, that is, the sender encrypts the message with a private key known only to the sender and receiver. However, public key cryptography is becoming more widely used as it has the advantage of using a public and private key pair, where the private key is only known to one party. A sender uses the recipients public key to encrypt data and on receipt the recipient uses their private key to decrypt the data.

In the EDIFACT world this is implemented using the rules for confidentiality, which are defined in ISO 9735 part 7

5.1.1.2 Repudiation

In the case of written documents, both parties signing a contract in the presence of witnesses ensures that neither party can repudiate entering into the contract. With electronic communication different methods have to be used.

Non repudiation of sender is ensured by using digital signatures. A digital signature uses a private key to sign an abstract algorithmically derived from the data within a message. As only the originator will be using their private key, the ability to decode it using the corresponding public key verifies the originator as its source. By storing the message with the originator's public key for auditing, the recipient has evidence of its provenance.

For non repudiation of receipt to work, the recipient must send an acknowledgement also digitally signed. A legal agreement by both parties on the use of the digital signatures reduces the possibility of litigation about the method.

In EDIFACT this is implemented using the AUTACK message which is defined in ISO 9735 part 6.

5.1.1.3 Masquerading

Because the two trading parties are separated at the time of the transaction, EDI (or any electronic communication) lends itself to masquerading. In normal life there is a reliance on physically recognising the other party and/or a hand-written signature being unique to reduce the risk of someone masquerading as someone else. With EDI there is a reliance on the digital signature to authenticate the originator and recipient.

As only the originator's private key can generate their digital signature, holders of the originator's public key cannot themselves generate a valid signature, so preventing the recipient claiming to have received a message that the sender did not generate.

This is fine for identifying the originator, as there is only one private key, but there may be several copies of the public key in circulation. There is, therefore, a possibility of one recipient masquerading as another. This can be prevented by ensuring a message only goes to the rightful recipient, and/or the use of the recipient's private key to generate a digitally signed acknowledgement for every signed message received (as for non-repudiation of receipt).

The use of Trusted Third Parties to provide certification of the public keys is another important measure in preventing masquerading.

In many ways EDI is more secure than other electronic communications methods that rely on paper output. For example, it is relatively easy to scan someone's signature and append it to a fax. Changing the stored Station Identifier in the fax machine can also lend credence to a false fax.

In EDIFACT this is implemented using the USH/UST envelope that is defined in ISO 9735-5, together with the AUTACK message.

5.1.1.4 Modification
Changing a document, such as a cheque, for financial gain is not unknown in the paper-based world, so it is to be expected with EDI transactions. By increasing or decreasing an amount in an EDI monetary field, or by changing the name of the payee, certain parties could stand to gain. Deleting a valid message sent to or by a competitor or ex-employer could prevent that organisation receiving an order, or receiving payment for an invoice. By using digital signatures and signed acknowledgements, both of these cases can be detected and prevented, but this can only be as good as the internal controls. Multiple digital signatures may improve internal controls.

Sending the same invoice, say, twice to the same partner could cause double payment to be made, even though the message is valid as far as the digital signature is concerned. However, EDIFACT itself has facilities to prevent this. If a message is really a duplicate then a duplicate indicator will be set (so it is no longer an exact duplicate) and the receiving application will be 'aware' that the message should not be processed twice.
The security header, USH, itself contains a sequence number, and every message has a unique mandatory message reference number. The application should check

that messages not marked as duplicates, do not have identical sequence numbers or message reference numbers. An optional timestamp can be used to determine that two messages were not transmitted at the same time – belt and two pairs of braces.

5.1.1.5 Fraud
Most of the examples given above have been concerned with deliberate attempts at fraud. The first line of defence is to prevent the fraud by security mechanisms provided by the EDI system. These do not, however, guard against fraud outside the EDI system, in that a fraudulently produced invoice, for example, sent through a secure EDI system will be validly signed and protected against repudiation. It is up to the receiving system to detect that the invoice is for goods that have not been delivered. This is outside the scope of this document.

5.1.2 EDIFACT Security

Having detailed the threats and the methods of dealing with them, the EDIFACT mechanisms for applying those methods deserve a mention.

The accepted way of applying security to EDIFACT messages is to add an envelope to the data within standard messages. After the normal message header and before the first element of user data is the security header segment, the USH. This header contains details of the security techniques used in that message, who signed it and a security sequence number to prevent duplication. At the end of the user data is the security trailer, the UST. (cf UNH and UNT for the message header and trailer.) This carries the digital signature to protect the preceding data.

To provide confidentiality, the user data inside the security envelope is encrypted, which produces a structureless binary file, filtered to convert it into text strings, and put into a CIPHER message as free text segments to put it back into EDIFACT format and allow it to pass through traditional EDI systems.

For non-repudiation, an acknowledgement and authentication message, AUTACK, has been defined.

Electronic data interchange Message Development Guide

This carries a copy of the originator's digital signature, itself protected by the recipients digital signature. Providing security at the message level has several advantages:

- sensitive, secured, messages can be mixed with less sensitive messages in the same interchange, thus reducing the overhead of unnecessarily securing ordinary messages

- when CIPHER is used, all the message information is hidden, including message type, so intelligence cannot be gathered about the details of messages going to a particular location. This might be important in government/military circles where purchase orders for snow shoes or malaria tablets, for example, could give intelligence to foreign governments about possible troop movements, including possible numbers involved. Traffic flow analysis may, however, provide intelligence if the recipient only manufactures snow shoes, but that is outside the scope of this document

- overhead is low compared to message size, but would be high if implemented at the smaller segment or data element levels.

Some users, mainly in the health sector, argue that only certain segments contain sensitive information, so only they should be encrypted, thus bringing encryption down to segment group, segment or lower levels. As the whole message must be secured with digital signatures anyway, it is arguable that this latter case would be over-engineering the solution to the problem.

Another argument is that encryption should apply to the whole data stream, using link level encypherment, but that precludes using EDI networks as they rely on (unencrypted) header data for routing and audit.

The standards defined for EDIFACT security at time of writing are:

- *ISO9735 part 5, Security (authenticity, integrity and non-repudiation)*

- *ISO9735 part 6, Secure Authentication and Acknowledgement Message (message type AUTACK)*

- *ISO9735 part 7, Security (Confidentiality) for batch EDI.*

These documents specify the way security is applied to EDIFACT messages, but not the encryption algorithms to be used. The security methods for interactive EDI have yet to be finalised.

5.1.2.1 Key Management
Where there are few trading partners, public keys can be simply exchanged by each of the trading partners. With larger communities, public keys are generally administered by a 'trusted third party', an organisation such as a bank or government department which ensures legally binding agreements exist on the use of public keys. The overheads of key management should not be underestimated.

5.1.3 Network Security

The popularity of VAN's is often attributed to their perceived security. Being closed and using PSTN circuits, they argue, prevents unauthorised users gaining access to the data being transmitted. Because VAN providers are commercial organisations, the user will have a contract with them, which will normally provide some legal protection against loss of revenue.

As VAN's become bigger, and in some cases, move their switching centres 'offshore', it becomes more possible that they could be penetrated for commercial espionage purposes.

In this respect VAN's must be assessed against known threats and vulnerabilities, taking due note at personnel and physical security issues. Network security is only a matter of degree when comparing public networks.

5.2 Legal

5.2.1 UNCID Rules

The United Nations Uniform Rules Of Conduct For Interchange Of Trade Data By Teletransmission (UNCID) lay down guidelines for the legal status of EDIFACT messages. Although of academic interest when designing messages in the abstract, these rules

Electronic data interchange Message Development Guide

must be remembered when designing for certain business environments. The full rules are available as part of SITPRO's EDIFACT Service.

The following extract is an example of the UNCID rules that apply to message design:

> Article 6: Messages and transfers
>
> a) A trade data message may relate to one or more trade transactions and should contain the appropriate identifier for each transaction and means of verifying that the message is complete and correct according to the TDI-AP concerned.
>
> b) A transfer should identify the sender and the recipient; it should include means of verifying, either through the technique used in the transfer itself or by some other manner provided by the TDI-AP concerned, the formal completeness and authenticity of the transfer.

Figure 14: Extract from UNCID Rules

5.2.2 Interchange Agreement

The use of EDI between trading partners is usually agreed beforehand, and must be as contractually secure as any trading agreement. To this end an Interchange Agreement is usually used by the business partners as a statement of the terms governing the conduct of the parties in exchanging EDI messages. The Electronic Commerce Association publishes such a Standard Electronic Data Interchange Agreement. A European version has been produced as part of the TEDIS programme and there is an M.O.D. variant of the ECA Interchange Agreement

If they use the Standard Electronic Data Interchange Agreement, the parties are confirming their intention, when communicating by EDI, to be committed to each other and they cannot claim ignorance of the rules of behaviour, or that they do not accept them and are not bound by them.

A specimen copy of the ECA's Standard Interchange Agreement is included in 'The EDI Implementation Guide' in this series, or can be obtained from the Electronic Commerce Association.

5.2.3 VAT and EDI

Any message that is designed to carry invoice information is governed by 'The Requirements Regarding Computer Data Interchange Of Invoice For Value Added Tax Purposes In The United Kingdom', published by HM Customs and Excise. In brief these require:

- At least one month's notice in writing before the message becomes operational. This must be built into message implementation timescales

- The parties must trial the system and invite HM Customs and Excise to attend one or more of those trials. This may also affect timescales

- Significant changes to the system must be notified to them

- The following information has to be kept so must be allowed for in the message:

    (a) Full name and address of the recipient of the invoice file and the sender's name, address and VAT registration number;

    (b) the unique transmission reference, or other unique reference allocated to the invoice file, and the transmission date;

    (c) the total numbers and types of invoices (or other documents) on the file.

A copy of the rules is included in Appendix D

6 Message Development Examples

6.1 **Message Examples Introduction**

This Chapter shows, by illustration of real life examples, how the syntax and message structures in UN/EDIFACT work. An example of a completed document is given which is followed by the equivalent message shown as a character string and then broken down into segments for easy human readability.

6.2 **Illustration of a Commercial Invoice**

The document that follows is (Figure 15), an EDIFACT invoice message claiming payment for chemicals supplied by ICI United Kingdom to QUIMIGAL de Oporto, Portugal, under conditions agreed between the seller and the buyer.

INVOICE

Seller Tlx no 512345 ICI Chemicals and Polymers PO Box 90 Wilton Middlesborough England TS6 8JE	Invoice date and No. 21-04-91 75-064-H-227171 Other Referenes EDS 0633096		
Consignee Quimigal De Opporto Ave Sancho 3 Barreiro Portugal	Buyer (if other than consignee) Alphonso Schmidt AG Ave Infanti Santo Lisbon 4 Portugal Ref No 064-5787-1B		
	Country of origin of goods United Kingdom		
Transport details Shipped from Teeside to Barreiro per Bailey Freight Insured value DM 55735	Terms of delivery and payment Free delivered Barreiro Taxes & clearance unpaid Payment 60 days from date of invoice by telegraphic transfer to account no 123-4567 with Westland Bank, Frankfurt, D-6123 Quoting Ref. ABC-1234		
Shipping marks; 1 No. and kind of packages; Goods description (in full and/or in code) Container no. Temp 20–25 DEG C 1 demountable ISO container Alphon 50 Schmidt AG 064-5787-1B		Gross weight kg 18,440kg	Cube m2
Specification of commodities (in code and/or in full) 5013456000158 – Pure dried vacuum salt We hereby certify that the goods mentioned in this invoice are of British origin	Quantity 18,440kg	Unit Price DM 2.850 per kg Net wt	Amount DM 52554
	Packing	Included above	Not incl. above
	Freight		
	Other codes (Specify)		
	Insurance		
	Total invoice amount		**DM 52554**

Figure 15: Example of a paper Invoice

Chapter 6
Message Development Examples

The above invoice has been transcribed into a UN/EDIFACT invoice message containing twenty-eight segments (including the UNH and UNT segments). It should be read as a single string of characters (Figure 16).

UNH+INV001+INVOIC:1'BGM+380+75-064-H-227101+910421'NA+SU+5 0134 56000145:14++ICI CHEMICALS AND POLYMERS+PO BOX 90:WILTON+MIDDLESBOROUGH++TS68JE+GB' RFF+SS+EDS0633096'RFF+PO+ABC-1234'CTA+IC++512345:TL'FII+RB+123-5567+:::WESTLAND BANK:FRANKFURT'NAD + BY++ ALPHONSO SCHMIDT AG:AVE INFANTI SANTO:LISBON 4:PORTUGAL'RFF+CR+ 064-5787-1B'NAD+CN+++QUIMIGAL DE OPPORTO+AVE SANCHO 3+BARREIRO+++PT'CUX+DEM:IN'ALI+GB'PAT+01+++05:03:D:60++++PAYMENT 60 DAYS FROM INVOICE DATE BY TELEGRAPHICS TRANSFER TO: ACCOUNT NO 123-4566 QUOTE REF ABC-1234:WESTLAND BANK, FRANKFURT'PAI+OP++30+03'TDT+++10+++::BAILEY FREIGHT'LOC+9+::TEESIDE 'LOC+8+::BARREIRO'TOD+ 02++FCA: 22+10:::BARREIRO++TAXES AND CLEARANCE UNPAID'PAC+1++VP:IS'MEA+WT +04+KGM:18440'PCI++TEMP 20 -25 DEG C:ALPHONSO SCHMIDT AG:064-5787-1B 'UNS+D'LIN+++5013456000 158:VN++12:18440:KD+2.85:NW:1:KD'UNS+S'TMA+52554'FTX+CUS+++WE HEREBY CERTIFY THAT THE GOODS MENTIONED IN THIS INVOICE ARE OF BRITISH ORIGIN'VAL+2+55735:DEM'UNT+28 +INV001'

Figure 16: Example INVOIC message

To enable the message to be more easily understood, it has been broken into segments below, each segment followed by its segment name. As a further guide to understanding certain qualifiers have been identified and named (in some the full description in the codes directory is required to enable a full understanding of the meaning). The segments are from the UN/EDIFACT 90.1 directory set.
UNH+INV001+INVOIC:1'
Message Header
BGM+380+75-064-H-227101+910421'
Beginning of Message (qualifier 380 = commercial invoice)
NAD+SU+5013456000145:14++ICI CHEMICALS AND POLYMERS+PO BOX 90:WILTON+MIDDLESBOROUGH++TS6 8JE+GB'
Name and Address (qualifier SU = supplier)
RFF+SS+EDS0633096'
RFF+PO+ABC-1234'
Reference (qualifier SS = sellers reference number)
CTA+IC++512345:TL'
Contact Information (qualifier IC = information contact)
FII+RB+123-4567+:::WESTLAND BANK:FRANKFURT'

Electronic data interchange Message Development Guide

Financial Institution Information (qualifier RB = receiving financial institution)
NAD+BY++ALPHONSO SCHMIDT AG:AVE INFANTI SANTO:LISBON 4:PORTUGAL'
Name and Address (qualifier BY = buyer)
RFF+CR+064-5787-1B'
Reference Qualifier CR = customer reference number)
NAD+CN+++QUIMIGAL DE OPPORTO+AVE SANCHO 3+BARREIRO+++PT'
Name and Address (qualifier CN = consignee)
CUX+DEM:IN'
Currencies
ALI+GB'
Additional Information (GB is country of origin)
PAT+01+++05:03:D:60++++PAYMENT 60 DAYS FROM INVOICE DATE BY TELEGRAPHICS TRANSFER TO:ACCOUNT NO 123-4566 QUOTE REF ABC-1234:WESTLAND BANK, FRANKFURT'
Payment Terms Basis
PAI+OP++30+03'
Payment Instructions
TDT+++10+++::BAILEY FREIGHT'
Details of Transport
LOC+9+::TEESIDE'
LOC+8+::BARREIRO'
Place/Location Identification (9 = place/port of loading; 8 = place of destination)
TOD+02++FCA:22+10:::BARREIRO++TAXES AND CLEARANCE UNPAID'
Terms Of Delivery, 02 = despatch condition)
PAC+1++VP:IS'
Package
MEA+WT+04+KGM:18440'
Measurements (WT = weight)
PCI++TEMP 20-25 DEG C:ALPHONSO SCHMIDT AG+064-5787-1B'
Package Identification
UNS+D'
Section Control
LIN+++5013456000158:VN++12:18440:KD+2.85:NW:1:KD'
Line Item
UNS+S'
Section Control
TMA+52554'

Total Message Amounts
FTX+CUS+++WE HEREBY CERTIFY THAT THE
GOODS MENTIONED IN THIS INVOICE ARE OF
BRITISH ORIGIN'
Free Text
VAL+2+55735:DEM'
Valuation
UNT+28+INV001'
Message Trailer

6.3 Illustration of the Single European Market Declaration Message

The following documentation is part of the HM Customs and Excise Electronic Data Capture Service (EDCS) Trade Specification. That specification is the description of the method by which certain data on exports to other European community countries by the international trading community is sent to HMC&E. It has been especially designed to allow Intra-EC Trade Statistics, or VAT-EC Sales Lists, or both sets of data combined to be transmitted to the EDCS.

The message type (ie tag) is SEMDEC and it is based on the standard Customs Declaration (CUSDEC) message that is a much larger message.

Electronic data interchange Message Development Guide

The INTRASTAT Form

Following is an illustration of the paper document that would be used to collect Intra-EC Trade Statistics if there was no EDI method.

Figure 17: Intrastat Form

Chapter 6
Message Development Examples

6.3.1 Branching Diagram

The following is the SEMDEC Message branching diagram. It shows the structure of the message in UN/EDIFACT layout.

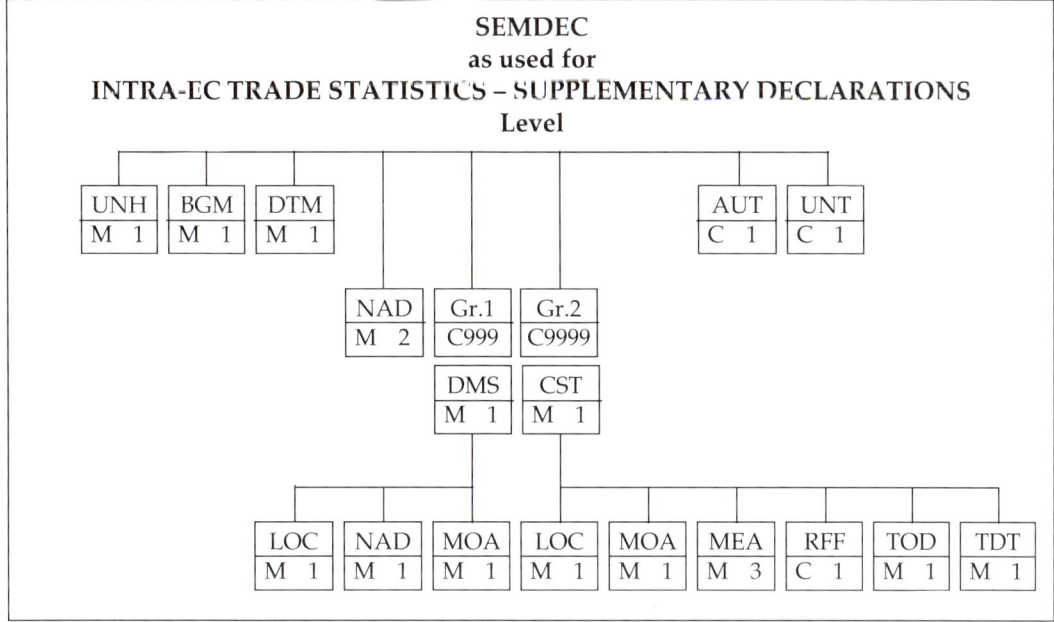

Figure 18: Intrastat Branching Diagram

The following diagram shows the data in a SEMDEC message as sent in a string of characters.

```
UNH+000004+SEMDEC:1:912:UK:109401'BGM+++137:930205:101'DTM+156:9301:609'NAD+DT+1
23456782'NAD+AE+342516769'CST++40141000:122+A:105+10:112'LOC+35:BE+27:BE'MOA+5+123
:100000'MEA+AAR++G13:1200'RFF+ABE:CND0001'TOD+++EXW'TDT+11++1'CST++88025000:12
2+A:105+10:112'LOC+35:FR'MOA+5+123:80000001'MEA+AAR++G13:750000'RFF+ABE:RCK0002'
TOD+++EXW'TDT+11++1'CST++31010000:122+D:105+20:112'LOC+36:IE'MOA+5+123:1'MEA+A
AR++G13:100000'MEA+WfB++NMB:3'TOD+++EXW'TDT+11++1'CST++38030000:122+D:105+20:
112'LOC+36:IE'MOA+5+123:25000'MEA+AAR++G13:1'RFF+ABE:OIL0004'TOD+++EXW'TDT+11
++1'CST++38030000:122+D:105+20:112'LOC+36:IE'MOA+5+123:25000'MEA+AAR++G13:3000000'
RFF+ABE:OIL0005'TOD+++EXW'TDT+11++1'CST++38030000:122+D:105+20:112'LOC+36:IE'MO
A+5+123:2500'MEA+AAR++G13:30000000'RFF+ABE:OIL0006'TOD+++EXW'TDT+11++1'UNT+49
+000004'
```

Figure 19: Intra-EC Trade Statistics – Supplementary Declarations

Electronic data interchange Message Development Guide

The segments above have been separated so that the message can be better appreciated:

UNH+000004+SEMDEC:1:912:UK:109401'
BGM+++137:930205:101'
DTM+156:9301:609'
NAD+DT+123456782'
NAD+AE+342516769'
CST++40141000:122+A:105+10:112'
LOC+35:BE+27:BE'
MOA+5+123:100000'
MEA+AAR++G13:1200'
RFF+ABE:CND0001'
TOD+++EXW'
TDT+11++1'
CST++88025000:122+A:105+10:112'
LOC+35:FR'
MOA+5+123:80000001'
MEA+AAR++G13:750000'
RFF+ABE:RCK0002'
TOD+++EXW'
TDT+11++1'
CST++31010000:122+D:105+20:112'
LOC+36:IE'
MOA+5+123:1'
MEA+AAR++G13:100000'
MEA+W-B++NMB:3'
TOD+++EXW'
TDT+11++1'
CST++38030000:122+D:105+20:112'
LOC+36:IE'
MOA+5+123:25000'
MEA+AAR++G13:1'
RFF+ABE:OIL0004'
TOD+++EXW'
TDT+11++1'
CST++38030000:122+D:105+20:112'
LOC+36:IE'
MOA+5+123:25000'
MEA+AAR++G13:3000000'
RFF+ABE:OIL0005'
TOD+++EXW'
TDT+11++1'
CST++38030000:122+D:105+20:112'
LOC+36:IE'

```
MOA+5+123:2500'
MEA+AAR++G13:30000000'
RFF+ABE:OIL0006'
TOD+++EXW'
TDT+11++1'
UNT+48+000004'
```

7 Software Development

7.1 The Translation Process

Data used in and by applications systems (such as financial accounting and order processing) needs to be transformed from the applications' data structures into the formalised data structures used in EDI. This process is often referred to as translation.

Therefore, at the core of any EDI software package is the translator function. Conceptually it is a two-stage process, and indeed it is often implemented as two entirely separate processes. One process – the parser – deals with all things EDI, primarily data compression and syntax and semantic checking. The other – the mapper – does the remainder of the transformation task.

The data interface between the parser and the mapper generally uses fixed-format records. That between applications and the mapper may either use a similar mechanism (especially where a suitable interface or print file already exists and has been reused for the EDI interface) or may use database views or structures familiar to the application itself.

It is important to note that most parsers can use the same message definition for both incoming and outgoing data. The data mapping requirements, however, will almost always need to be specified separately for each direction.

7.1.1 'Parsing'

EDI formats generally have to meet two major constraints; the positional nature of data elements within segments (and sub-items within composite items) must be maintained, but the number of characters to be transmitted has to be minimised. Thus, for the majority of commonly used EDI syntax standards, trailing spaces in alphanumeric fields and insignificant leading and trailing zeros in numeric data are suppressed, and segments and composite items are truncated to the last non-blank field.

The complexity of the compression process to produce variable-format output, coupled with the associated need to perform syntax and semantic checks, means that usually the data interface to the parser is in the form of

Electronic data interchange Message Development Guide

fixed-format files, where (eg for EDI output) one input record to the parser equates to one output segment and where each data element that might be present has its maximum size. The parser can then concentrate on the compression and syntax checking functions.

The natural consequence of this is that a separate process (often called 'mapping') is needed to provide the link between applications systems and the parser interface files. (See following section.)

The compression aspects of the parser have already been described; removal (following the appropriate syntax rules) of trailing spaces in alphanumeric fields and insignificant leading and trailing zeros in numeric data, and truncating segments and composite items to the last non-blank field. (And, of course, the opposite process for incoming data.)

The syntax issues, however, are much more complex.

7.1.2 Syntax Checking

The parser is the logical place at which to implement syntactic checks, both for compliance with the EDI standard and conformance to a bilateral or partnership agreement. The two criteria may be mutually contradictory, in which case conformance normally takes precedence.

The following is a non-exhaustive list of checks that might be automatically imposed by the parser. It should be remembered, though, that in the case of outgoing data, instead of checking a condition or value the parser may be called upon to generate the condition or value, and this can be one of the most complex areas of parser design.

Within a transmission, for each interchange;

- EDI standard/envelope type known. The arrival of an interchange in an unknown or unexpected EDI syntax, or containing an unknown or unexpected document type, should result in immediate rejection of the interchange

- Trading partner valid, standard correct. The EDI envelope will contain the sender details. An unknown sender, or invalid combination of sender, message type and EDI standard, should again result in immediate rejection of the interchange

- Valid destination. Where the communications mechanism does not impose these checks, it must be ensured that the envelope is addressed to the recipient, and destined for a valid location within the organisation.

Within an envelope,

- Envelope trailer counts and control numbers match (see note 1 below). This is a simple check that the envelope contains the correct number of functional groups (batches) or messages, and that the end-of-envelope label has the same identity as the start-of-envelope label. It is the highest level of control against data corruption during transmission

- Message type valid from trading partner. Not all trading partners may send all message types, so that the installation will accept invoices from one partner does not necessarily mean that another partner (from whom other documents are accepted) may also send invoices

- Standard, version correct. This check detects changes by partners adopting revised syntaxes that might otherwise lead to the data being incorrectly interpreted.

Within a functional group or batch,

- Valid destination. Ensure that the functional group is destined for a valid location within our organisation

- Message type valid from trading partner. (Functional groups, where used, can contain only one type of message)

- Batch trailer counts and control numbers match (see note 1). This is a simple check that the functional group (batch) contains the correct number of messages, and that the end-of-functional-group label has the same identity as the start label. It is the second level of control against data corruption during transmission.

Within a message,

- Message type valid from trading partner (as above)

- Message trailer counts and control numbers match (see note 1 below). This is a simple check that the message contains the correct number of segments, and that the end-of-message label has the same identity as the start label. It is the third level of control against data corruption during transmission

- All segments belong to message and appear in correct sequence

- Presence of all mandatory segments

- Segment maximum repeat count not exceeded

- Segment group (loop) maximum repeat count not exceeded

- Count of repeats of a given segment or group (loop) correct

- 'Hash' totals correct. This is the lowest level of control against data corruption during transmission, where critical values are 'summed' to produce a verifiable hash total.

Within a segment,

- Mandatory data item presence correct

- Composite data item composition correct

- Data item/sub-item minimum and maximum length within permitted range

- Data item type (eg numeric is numeric)

- ID data type against its code list (but only for primitive elements; it excludes multi-part codes where, for example, the first two bytes are from one code list and the next three from another. These are being actively discouraged and discontinued by ANSI, the only standards body to use this construct)

- Conditional inter-relationships among items valid, either within the segment or among elements of a composite, ie

    P   (Paired or Multiple, all_or_none) – if any of the listed items is present then all must be present

    R   (Required, at_least_one) – one or more of the items listed must be present

    E   (Exclusion, one_or_none) – only one of the items listed may be present (but it is permissible that none are present)

    C   (Conditional, one_and_all) – if the first item listed is present, then all the remaining listed items must be present also (but any or all of the listed items NOT specified as the FIRST may appear without requiring that the first item be present). The order of the dependent items need not be the order in which they appear in the segment.

    L   (List Conditional, one_and_some) – if the first item listed is present, then at least one of the remaining listed items must be present also (but any or all of the listed items NOT specified as the FIRST may appear without requiring that the first item be present). The order of the dependent items need not be the order in which they appear in the segment.

- Data item values match static or calculated value. 'Hash' totals are one such check. Another is the case where, within ANSI messages, some segments other than message trailers must contain counts of the number of occurrences of another segment or loop. A final example is commonplace, occurring in almost all EDI standards, where a segment includes a data element containing an iteration number of that segment within its loop, and sometimes this is nested within hierarchical repeats.

Note 1. Different EDI standards impose different rules for the construction of envelope, functional group and message control numbers. These are flexible enough to allow different trading partners to take different views, and to impose different requirements. For example, one partner may require that envelope control numbers are sequential for each trading partner, whereas another may generate a single sequence of control numbers regardless of recipient. Clearly, these partners will encounter problems. For this and other related reasons, it is generally best to equip the software with the capability of generating control numbers based on the recipient, and so responsibility for this function normally falls upon the parser.

The parser should be able to implement compliance with the standard, as varied by different conformance requirements. Many checks need, therefore, to be applied independently for a particular version and variant of the message. The term variant is used to indicate the requirements of complying with a bilateral partnership or trading group convention, which may or may not breach compliance, and version to indicate a particular issue of the standard or message from the message authority.

While most such versions and variants can be determined from the message descriptors contained in the EDI data itself, sometimes the same variant and version will be used in different ways by different partners. To deal with this case, the parser should optionally be able to assume a particular variant on a per trading partner basis, based solely on the message type and the sender-ID.

Another advantage of these checks being configurable according to trading partner is to give improved parser performance, where the degree of confidence is high, and a reduction in the degree of checking over time is natural in a trading relationship.

It may also be possible, but not necessarily recommended, to dispense with some of the checks for a particular message by omitting or deleting these checks from the message definition. Segment count checks, control number matches, hash totals, inter-item conditionality checks and code-list checks sometimes fall into this category.

7.1.3 Miscellaneous Points

Most modern EDI syntaxes allow for the possibility of changing the delimiters used to separate composite elements and items within segments, to mark the decimal point, and to terminate segments. They also allow for an 'escape' character, which restores the immediately following character to its natural meaning rather than its delimiter meaning. (Eg the most commonly used item separator is the plus character, "+". To send the text string "A + B" so that it is interpreted correctly, the escape character might be defined"?", so in an EDI message our string might appear as "A ?+ B".)

Therefore, any EDI software must cope with both requirements.

Finally, there is generally a requirement to be able to re-send data. While in many cases this merely means retrieving the previously sent data from an archive and sending it again, some EDI syntaxes (notably TRADACOMS) require actual changes to data elements within the message to show that the data has been re-transmitted. It is a moot point whether the responsibility for making these changes falls to the EDI software or the application that produced the data in the first place.

7.1.4 Defining New Messages

It is possible to write programs that deal specifically with a particular message in a particular EDI syntax. The obvious drawback with such programs is that as the message evolves over time through different versions, then the programs have to change. Clearly, with only a few messages in several versions, maintenance becomes difficult, and eventually impossible to co-ordinate. It is much more usual to write 'table-driven' parsers, where the program adapts to different EDI syntaxes, messages, and their versions and variants by loading and interpreting different tables. The small overhead in loading and interpreting these tables is more than made up for by the generality of the solution, the fact that only a single program has to be maintained, and the commercial availability of sophisticated GUI-based tools for reviewing the messages published by national and international standards bodies and automatically converting these into the required tables.

7.1.5   Diagnostics

It can be most useful, especially to the novice EDI user, to have the parser print out what it is seeing and doing as it parses the EDI data. It is not always apparent to even an experienced user what data items in a segment are and what they mean, but in general the parser knows in detail what it is processing. This facility, if provided by the parser, can be especially useful for expanding coded values for ease of understanding, and for diagnosing bad data constructions, which can often happen with novice users or when new document types are being trialled.

7.1.6   Data Mapping

The inputs and outputs to the mapping process are best viewed as records and fields. The records that comprise the interface between the mapper and parser often correspond closely to the segment definitions used in the particular EDI message being used. Those between the mapper and the application may be real records or virtual records derived from a database view, but for simplicity both will be referred to here as plain records.

The sorts of transformations carried out by the mapper between input records and output records are:

- copy a field in an input record to a field in an output record

    - change the field format (eg numeric becomes alpha)

    - change the field size (eg extend/truncate)

    - provide default value if input field is empty

    - source for an output field can be dependent on value in another field

- use the value in the input to derive a value in the output (by computation or by table lookup)

    - option to specify default if the lookup fails

- insert arbitrary values in the output

    - preset values or text

    - value obtained from a database

    - values provided by the system, eg run date, start time, time now, running numbers, counts

    - totalling or other computation

However, these are only field-to-field operations. There are other record-to-record operations that the mapping software must perform.

Because of the way EDI data is exchanged in segments, often data from a number of segments need to be assembled into a single application system record or vice versa.

Input records, therefore, need to be buffered in memory by the mapper so that

- it is possible for more than one output record to contain data elements from the same input record, and

- one output record can contain data elements from several input records.

It may also be necessary, for example, to send both the original value and a lookup derived from it in different output records, eg the recipient's ANA number in the UNB envelope header, with the customer details in another segment which will probably come from the customer number field in the application system's header record.

It is also possible for records to be copied directly from input to output. This is especially useful in artificial

Electronic data interchange Message Development Guide

mapping processes used to channel input data in several directions, eg where it is required to copy records to different output files depending on some criterion of the input, such as whether the customer is EDI capable or not.

Some mapping processes can also write several output files simultaneously, each with its own format. One use of this facility might be to write an output file of transformed invoice data, and a second file listing, say, the invoice numbers and customers to whom they were sent.

So referring to the earlier example, if some recipients were EDI capable and some not, the data file could change so that the mapping process produced one file for EDI and one to print, but the file of invoice numbers and receiving customers would remain the same.

With data mapping processes there are always some prerequisites and restrictions and it must be accepted that, no matter how sophisticated the mapping process, it is not feasible in every case to automatically transform one file format into another in a single process.

As a simple example, consider the case of the purchase order. Suppose for a moment that in a purchase order application system, the designer chose to base the design on commodities, so for each commodity there is an associated list of order lines that need to be fulfilled. The database has been optimised with this view in mind and printed orders contain a list of products, with for each product a list of locations to which the product should be delivered.

While this makes life easy for manufacturing and purchasing, for shipping there is a need to sort the data by destination, so that each shipping document has, within each location, a list of the products to be shipped there.

The common EDI standards for purchase orders often allow either commodity or location-based ordering, so in dealing with a customer or supplier who has taken the opposite view to one's own, at least a sort process will need to be included, and possibly more complex processing, to invert the data.

7.2 Communications Management

Up to this point, the guide has concentrated on the technology to generate or accept data as an EDI message. However, this is of no use unless the EDI messages can be sent to or received from trading partner(s).

The essential requirement is the ability to send and receive EDI messages. This usually translates into the ability to send and receive files, the domain of the file transfer protocol. (For the purposes of this discussion the use of magnetic media for file transfer is discounted, although this is perfectly sound for large data volumes where time is not of the essence, and confine ourselves to the requirements of communications-based file transfer.)

7.2.1 Protocols

There are two main sorts of protocol used for file transfer today; point-to-point and store-and-forward. Examples of point-to-point protocols are legion, but some of the more widely used ones include 2780 (an originally IBM synchronous protocol), Kermit, Xmodem and its derivative Zmodem, OFTP (Odette File Transfer Protocol) and FTP (which additionally requires a transport layer protocol like TCP/IP, PPP or SLIP).

The most common store-and-forward protocol is X.400, although most E-mail systems fall into the store-and-forward category.

Depending on the actual file transfer protocol used, it may be necessary to structure the data to be transferred in a particular way. Two examples are included here. The first concerns 2780 type protocols (including 3270 and 3780) where the protocol assumes files to be transferred have a record structure with a predetermined record size. To use these protocols for EDI, it is conventional to 'wrap' the EDI data so that the data runs from record to record in a continuous stream, eg the EDIFACT data:

UNB+UNOA:1+01010000602001+01010000589001+901004:0405+30071810040405++INVOICES'
UNH+1+INVOIC:88:1:UN:INVCON'
BGM+380+CB 038074300718+901003++MC2955:DP+901003'

```
RFF+PO+D5000231650307'
NAD+SU++RSS:P.O.BOX 14:MEADOWHALL
RD:SHEFFIELD:S9 1ED'
CTA+AD++0742 560152:TE'
NAD+DP++CEMENTATION PILING & FDNS:PHASE
2B:HIGH ST:WATFORD:ACCESS VIA LOATS LANE'
CUX+GBP'
UNS+D'
```

might appear 'wrapped' to 40-characters wide as:

```
UNB+UNOA:1+01010000602001+01010000589001
+901004:0405+30071810040405++INVOICES'UN
H+1+INVOIC:88:1:UN:INVCON'BGM+380+CB 038
074300718+901003++MC2955:DP+901003'RFF+P
O+D5000231650307'NAD+SU++RSS:P.O.BOX 14:
MEADOWHALL RD:SHEFFIELD:S9 1ED'CTA+AD++0
742 560152:TE'NAD+DP++CEMENTATION PILING
 & FDNS:PHASE 2B:HIGH ST:WATFORD:ACCESS
VIA LOATS LANE'CUX+GBP'UNS+D'LIN+000001+
```

The second example is comparatively widespread, and involves inserting into the data file commands that will be actioned by the communications software, eg

```
RECIPIENT: XYZ COMPANY
SENDER: ABC COMPANY
DATA:
<the actual data to be sent is included here>
$$$$
```

7.2.2 Communications issues

If a point-to-point protocol is being used then one or other party calls the other (who must be listening for the call), transfers data and hangs up. The only things that need to be agreed are who will call whom and when and, so long as the file transfer protocol is robust, there is no question about whether or not a file has been received.

As the early pioneers found, when communicating with more than one trading partner using a point-to-point protocol, there is a problem concerning timing. The receiver must either be constantly listening, and have enough channels to answer the maximum number of simultaneous calls he will receive, or a schedule must be agreed between all parties, which rapidly becomes impossible to co-ordinate and to adjust and compensate for failures.

As technology progresses and processor power moves ever upward, the problem of simultaneous sessions has become easier to overcome, and the cost of a bank of modems or a wide-band connection has fallen to the point where point-to-point file transfer is now a feasible option, so long as the partners can agree on the file transfer protocol itself. However, communications is still a complex discipline, and where there are many partners it may still be outside the capabilities of even quite large companies to provide the necessary service.

Store-and-forward protocols avoid the need for the recipient to be available whenever the sender wants to send, by making use of a 'message store'. If the recipient is not available, messages sent to him are 'buffered' in the message store and passed on when he is next available. (A simple example is the telephone answering machine.) Either the recipient calls in and accesses the store, or the mere fact that he comes on-line triggers the automatic transfer of stored messages, depending on the sophistication of the system.

Such protocols have advantages in some cases:

- if the message store is remote to the user, then the communications channel and its software need not be open and running all the time

- there are fewer security issues with regard to remote access to the company's computer systems.

When the concept of a message store is introduced, then another problem arises; the message store must be maintained by a service to which the sender must also have access.

There are essentially two sorts of store-and-forward environment; wide area messaging services such as E-mail and X400, and the Value Added Network Providers, or VANs. In neither case is there necessarily any assurance of being able to reach a particular trading partner, and there is always the possibility that there will be a need to subscribe to more than one such service.

Electronic data interchange Message Development Guide

Check the availability of interconnects (a mechanism by which one provider connects to another provider to allow messages to be delivered to the end recipient, either as a free or premium rate service).

In addition to electronic mailboxes, VANs offer a number of services such as:

- simple connections using point-to-point protocols, with local 'points of presence' to reduce communications costs

- security by validation of trading relationships – only the types of documents specified from the named sender can be received

- security checks against masquerading

- guaranteed integrity of data against snooping or tampering

- translation – of character set, message format or even EDI standard

- reporting – when messages arrive in the sender's or receiver's mailbox, or when they are extracted

- storage – in case of the need to re-extract or as an adjunct to or replacement for on-site archiving

- capacity – as many simultaneous connections as needed

- support for multiple protocols

- breaking an envelope containing multiple different functional groups into individual document types for selective extraction

- options to prioritise processing by extracting only messages of a particular kind, or from a particular trading partner

- option to have the VAN call out, and deliver data, when data is placed in the mailbox by a trading partner

- consultancy skills

- data entry and printing services, for companies not yet EDI capable.

VANs do, however, charge for their services, and the costs of these facilities must be weighed against the advantages they offer. Also, the types of services and the service levels offered vary from VAN to VAN, not always in ways directly related to their cost.

Modern file transfer protocols generally work properly or not at all. Although transmission failure and recovery for a failed session, and a method for dealing with each, must be considered, data corruption caused by transmission errors, which plagued early implementors, does not generally have to be dealt with. However, where a store-and-forward mechanism is used, there needs to be some sort of end-to-end response, to give the sender reassurance that the message did ultimately arrive at its destination.

VANs provide this reassurance in terms of mailbox and postbox reports, a service for which the user pays, but generally only where both the sender and recipient subscribe to the same VAN. Where this is not the case, it is generally safer for the partners to agree to exchange end-to-end responses by way of 'functional acknowledgements'. (As a point of terminology, a postbox is where outgoing messages are placed, which the VAN then transfers to partners' mailboxes. A mailbox is where messages awaiting collection or delivery are held.)

Wide area messaging services normally offer delivery notification and/or receipt advice as part of the service, but generally it is up to the sender to request it, and although there is only an honour obligation on the recipient to comply in most cases such systems work robustly and well.

Electronic data interchange Message Development Guide

7.2.3 Summary

To summarise the issues, communications and communications management software must be able to:

- prepare EDI files for transmission (eg 'wrapped' records, special headers/footers, commands for communications software)

- maintain queue of outbound files (by partner if point-to-point, by VAN or WAN if not)

- provide timed communications session (to take advantage of off-peak tariffs)

- implement the chosen file transfer protocol, for which appropriate software and hardware will be required, with at least one channel (for connection to VAN) or possibly more for point-to-point working

- record the success or failure of the transmission

- provide the capability to re-send or re-extract data

- record expectation of end-to-end response, and alert if it does not arrive in the specified time.

From the software design point of view, there are two options; design the software to expect one communications method, and re-write it when the method changes or it is necessary to communicate with a partner for whom the method is inappropriate, or write a generic interface which could drive many different communications methods and add them from third-party vendors.

7.2.4 Other Important Issues

Beware that some communications solutions may meet the short-term need but limit a company's options in the longer term. These solutions may reflect badly upon the company if they limit the options of its partners or unduly increase their costs. Factors to be considered include:

- if this communications protocol is adopted with this partner/VAN, will it be usable later with other partners/VANs?

- if subscribed to this service to reach this partner, can the same service be used to reach other partners, and at what cost?

- by forcing a trading partner to use a particular service, is that a restriction of their options in the future, will there be resentment, and does it matter?

Also be aware that the company will come to depend upon electronic transfer of data, and loss of capability should be included as a part of the disaster plan. Temporary interruptions of communications service are if not routine then at least fairly common, and it is useful to have a fallback mechanism. The communications management function should routinely try the backup mechanism or alternate routing if one exists.

7.3 Controlling and Auditing

There are several ways in which EDI can be initiated, so it is necessary to choose the methods most appropriate to the data volumes that will be processed with EDI, and the way in which the business uses or produces the data.

- Interactively by an operator

- Automatically as a result of output from applications systems

- Externally, triggered by the arrival of an incoming data transfer

- Automatically at time-of-day.

In all but the last case auditing and recovery are much simplified, since there is an immediate indication of whether the process was successful, and often the opportunity to re-try a failed communications session there and then.

Where a connection is to be made automatically at time of day (or, indeed, several times per day) then the process must of necessity be more complex. Some sort of queue must be maintained of events to be undertaken at the next connection, and there must be a mechanism for requesting operator action in the event that automatic recovery is not possible. The communications system becomes, in effect, autonomous, and operates asynchronously with the other systems elements.

In all cases, the software should:

- maintain an archive copy of all data sent and received for a reasonable period, taking into account legislative requirements and partnership issues

- record what data was sent and to whom, and record (where facilities are available for this) that the data has arrived at its destination, when, whether it has been formally acknowledged, etc

- record what data was received and from whom, and whether or not it has been formally acknowledged

- provide housekeeping facilities to clean up this archive and reporting data when it has served its purpose.

The requirements of the control systems will vary in line with the degree of automation to be achieved. At the simplest level, the operator will interactively take files of data exported by applications, invoke the translation function and then use the communications function to send the data, taking manual recovery actions in case of failure. For incoming data, files retrieved from a mailbox may be submitted to the inbound translator and then an applications system invoked to deal with the received data. Where the need for EDI is infrequent or of low volume or value, this mechanism may be all that is required.

At the other end of the scale, many applications systems on a distributed corporate computing environment may be continually producing data and submitting it to an EDI function which is automatically digesting the data, sorting it by recipient and taking appropriate mapping, translation and communications actions on the data, and reporting back to the originating application on the progress of its task and the eventual disposition of the data. Such an EDI function might also be capable of invoking an applications system to deal with received data after it had been through EDI pre-processing, or perhaps merely placing the data in a receiving location for the application to process on its next routine invocation.

The sophistication of the functions required and the level of integration with existing applications systems is beyond the scope of this guide. In general, the more facilities an EDI product has, the more opportunity there will be for co-operation between applications systems and the EDI function, and for automation of these linkages.

8 Testing

The main difference between EDI and other software projects is that it requires a close working relationship with third parties who have their own priorities, timescales and resource limitations. These both differ from the designer's and are resistant to external control, so achieving success is time-intensive and may defy normal project control methods.

This section, therefore, sets out to specify the steps that need to be taken and their interdependencies, but more importantly it makes suggestions as to what can be worked on during unavoidable delays, and indeed, how external delays can be used to good effect to further ensure reliability and correctness of those elements over which the user has total control.

The suggestions are relevant both to home-grown EDI solutions and to commercial EDI packages bought to work alongside existing applications.

NOTE. In what follows the word translation will be used to refer to the entire process of data mapping and EDI message construction (and vice versa for incoming transfers) and the word translator to refer to the software that accomplishes this.

8.1 General Notes

Test plans must include error conditions. The test plans should try to recreate as many permutations as is realistic given the time constraints. All plans should include syntax checking of messages sent and received. The plans should gradually extend to more complex, multiple message conversations. There should be deliberate testing to force syntax errors, and deviations from the protocol stated in the service agreement should also be tested.

8.2 Correctness of Application Data

The idea of determining whether or not the applications are up to the task of doing EDI, while not strictly a testing issue, is nevertheless an important first consideration. One of the of the primary causes of failure in EDI implementation is the quality of the data in the applications system. The activity of checking existing data and putting right any deficiencies is completely independent of the EDI experience, although changes or additions will often have to be made to reflect the requirements of EDI.

Particularly important are areas such as customer data, location codes, product codes, and anything in which an error would not matter when the data were acted on by a human but would be incorrect or produce the wrong results when processed by a computer. (Humans are very good at saying 'Oh, of course he means A when he says B, so I'll act accordingly.' In an EDI environment this inherent error recovery capability is lost.)

This review task can meaningfully start as soon as the decision is made to adopt EDI, since it is almost certain that applications systems data will be found to be inadequate, in the wrong format, or just plain wrong. Then, almost as soon as the first sample EDI data is obtained or the partner specification arrives, other inadequacies will be uncovered, and the more EDI messages that are contemplated, the more errors and omissions will be found.

Decisions will have to be made about whether to add to the application data structures data elements that are not currently present but are needed for EDI, and whether to change internal codes, or use cross-reference tables during the data mapping stage. If the latter, then creation and maintenance of these tables must be planned for, and the creation and maintenance routines tested.

It is often convenient to let the EDI package insert the odd data item (eg VAT number, own EDI Identity with respect to trading partners) but the location and method required to change these items periodically must be tested and must not be left undocumented.

8.3 Applications Interfaces to Translation

Second only to correctness of applications system data, one of the primary impediments to the introduction of EDI is the lack of suitable interfaces for import to, and export from, applications systems. The most common type of interface is the so-called flat file approach, where the application writes an export file to be read by the EDI package (and accepts an import file from EDI package for incoming data). With suitable software, it may also be possible to export directly from a relational database, or to utilise existing export files (such as print files), perhaps with minor changes.

Assuming such interfaces exist (or are being constructed), having a selection of small test files to use will allow some interaction with the system before any other systems or agencies become involved.

If the application is exporting data, these files can be used to test the EDI data mappings into the translator (especially if the interfaces are being constructed and there is any delay in writing the extract routines from the applications), and can also be used as a cross-check that the export routine is providing data in the correct format with all expected data fields populated.

Where the application is importing, then having test files can allow the import to be tested independently of the EDI translator mapping, or to check that the mapping is providing data in the correct format with all expected data fields populated. A cross-check, with both an import and manual input of what should be identical data, will resolve any problems and allow correct documentation of the interfaces to be established.

8.4 Correctness of EDI Specification

The EDI specification describes the data that will be exchanged between partners and the meanings ascribed to each data element. The result of a detailed examination of the EDI specification and the applications system data formats will be a set of data relationships. Every data relationship should be double checked before data communication starts.

It can often be productive to obtain copies of actual messages being exchanged by others in similar circumstances. For example, if the proposed trading partner is sending and/or receiving messages already, try to obtain some actual representative EDI data. An industry trade association, such as the ECA, may also be able to help by putting the designer in touch with members using EDI in a similar way.

There are several reasons why this exercise can be useful. It will enable the specification to be compared with the messages, which will pinpoint discrepancies between theory and practice, and misunderstandings caused by lack of familiarity. Not all operational changes make it into the documentation, and interpretation of what was intended in the specification is much enhanced by having a live example.

Where practical examples cannot be obtained from outside, then it will often be possible to create sample data using a simple text editor. (All EDI messages contain only character data – there are no packed-decimal or binary fields. Therefore, any character mode text editor will suffice for this task, but it does require at least some familiarity with the structure and format of EDI messages.)

If the EDI software has the capability to produce a diagnostic trace, put the test data through it. For those new to EDI, this can be an invaluable learning experience, and should make it much simpler to understand what data items are included in the message and what their values are, so that the actual message can be compared with the specification. As an example, consider this EDI message fragment:

STX=ANAA:1+5013546011325:TESCO STORES LTD+5010076000003:ET
SUTHERLAND& SONS +900703:153841+000001+PASSWORD+ORDTES'
MHD=1+ORDHDR:6'
TYP=0430+NEW-ORDERS'
etc.

A typical diagnostic output might be:

Start Of Segment	STX	
Identifier	1010	ANAA
Version	1011	1
Code	1020	5013546011325
Name	1021	TESCO STORES LTD
Code	1030	5010076000003
Name	1031	ET SUTHERLAND& SONS
Date of Transmission	1040	900703
Time of Transmission	1041	153841
Sender's transmission reference	1050	000001
Application Reference Only 6	1070	ORDTES
Start Of Segment	MHD	
Message reference seq'l in tr 1090		1
Type	1100	ORDHDR
Version Number	1101	6
Start Of Segment	TYP	
Transaction Code	4010	0430
Transaction Type	9010	NEW-ORDERS

8.5 Correctness of EDI Software

If use is being made of third-party software, then this step should be unnecessary. However, it is vital if the EDI software is being written in-house or comes from a provider who cannot demonstrate an established track record.

In selecting an EDI supplier, it is worthwhile spending time testing the provided maintenance routines and table creation utilities. A well-designed EDI interface will use tables for the specification of the EDI messages and data mappings. While the provider may well supply tables (either for free or at a cost), if there is likely to be a need to customise the tables for particular trading relationships, without involving the software provider, then becoming familiar with the interfaces is a necessity.

Electronic data interchange Message Development Guide

The data entered in these maintenance tables should match the published protocol for the messages to be implemented. Adherence to the agreed standard is fundamental to the success of the EDI application. If designers find themselves having to compromise the integrity of the EDI standard to meet the business need, then assume first that a mistake has been made and seek professional advice.

This activity can only be done before any contact with a trading partner if the message to be used is well established in the proposed trading community. Be aware, however, that some EDI users have taken a non-standard approach to message utilisation that may not match the industry norm. This does not mean that they are not complying with the appropriate EDI standards – merely that they have taken a different view on the way in which data elements are mapped into the EDI message.

8.6 Correctness of EDI Processing

For incoming EDI, the test data referred to above, can be passed through the translator and into the application to see what the effects will be long before there is any physical communication. For outgoing data, it can be used to ensure that the applications export and EDI mapping can produce similar-looking data, again without any actual communications. In both cases it provides a further check that the sample import/export test files were correct and, if not, allows problems to be identified early, the implications assessed and remedial action planned in good time.

Having a small file of test messages to use will also allow testing of some batch routines. It may be possible to provide entry points in the software for these messages to be inserted, providing a method of recreating the whole EDI conversion process or just testing small portions of it.

Checking the syntax and format of outgoing messages is also important. This can be done by viewing the outgoing data message before it reaches the communications module and leaves the local environment, and even before the communications capability exists. There should be some facility to view the composite messages in their ASCII format to facilitate this (normally suppressed during day-to-day use). A simple character-mode text editor will often suffice, but individual EDI segments may be several hundreds of characters long so be careful to select an editor that can cope with this.

Questions to ask about the outgoing data format include:

- Is the message correctly wrapped up with service-level segments?

- Is it addressed properly?

- Do the delimiter characters match the EDI protocol conventions?

- Are the numeric counters consistent when describing more than one item – for example, do they increment properly?

- Is all the text in upper case if it needs to be (eg for UNOA) or are the requirements of the chosen syntax being correctly met?

More general questions about the messages are:

- Will the message fail at the other end, for example, because numeric data is in alpha fields and vice versa?

- Have the data items been successfully mapped all the way from the application to the message?

- If surnames are used, are hyphenated ones and those with prefixes such as 'McAlpine' handled correctly?

- Have internal codes been translated into ISO/Industry equivalents correctly? (This is especially important if denominations of quantity are subtly different.) Have all cross-references and table look-ups been actioned correctly?

- Is there any conflict between special characters used for EDI delimiters and the data from the application?

Electronic data interchange Message Development Guide

Have any required escape characters been correctly inserted?

- In formatting a message it is sensible to reduce superfluous characters and delimiters to a minimum? This will cut transmission costs, speed processing and reduce the chance of data loss. These aspects of the generated messages should be checked.

8.7 EDI Interface to Communications

There is plenty that can to be done before a physical connection is made. In most cases there will be a facility to submit an EDI message for transmission later, and reporting facilities to see what is waiting to be sent where. Clearly, the act of submitting what would appear to be a correct message should result in data being correctly routed and queued. If it does not, it can be fixed by aborting the queue and re-creating it.

Many communications mechanisms are equipped with loopback capability, so it may be possible to simulate not only transmission but also (simultaneously) receipt, and so the incoming data path can also be tested. It is unusual to both send and receive the same sort of message, so loopback testing is often achieved by substituting the appropriate sort of test data either before the data is 'sent' or after it has been 'received'. Break points in the batch procedures can often be trivially engineered for this purpose.

(With this test, it may be necessary temporarily to configure the communications software to send a message type that will normally only be received and vice versa. In general, the cost of doing so is not onerous, and the benefits of loopback testing can be considerable.)

8.8 Correct Functioning of EDI Communications Channel

In establishing and trialling the initial communications connection, the communications initiator should be aware of the network address, security features and names to identify themselves to the recipient. This information should be entered in the service agreement and shared between both parties before the initial communications connection. Simple things, like ensuring both systems' clocks are accurate, should not be overlooked. Otherwise, messages to or from trading partners may be rejected unexpectedly.

The availability of sample EDI messages also means that this activity can be carried out separately from the other processing steps, for example, when the communications element has been installed but before the applications interface elements are ready, or even using a 'borrowed' communications module.

If the primary test is successful, some EDI messages can be sent and received immediately to prove the link is established at the application level. Performance figures should be obtained regarding data throughput and checks made to ensure that throughput is sufficient to meet the design objectives. Early identification of the fact that the data channel is inadequate will leave time for a revision if necessary, given the relatively long lead times on telecommunications equipment and lines.

Once confidence has been established, mechanical disruption of the communication channel (eg pulling the plug) should be tried to test resilience and error recovery. Of primary importance is verification that partially received files are deleted, and not allowed to go through to parsing, which they will inevitably fail. Also, that the files are correctly received in a subsequent communications session.

It must be remembered that manual procedures may be required to re-extract a file whose transfer failed previously, which may in some cases require intervention from the VAN helpdesk. The testing in this area must therefore establish that transfer failures are detected, that partial files are discarded, and that failing files can subsequently be retrieved (either automatically or by manual intervention, and if the latter that the procedures are well documented).

Circumstances can arise where data is lost (for example, where the VAN does no archiving and once the file is apparently retrieved it is deleted and gone forever). It is important here to test the partner's and one's own capability to re-generate the lost messages and re-send them.

8.9   End-to-End Testing

Simple end-to-end testing involves validating the link between the trading partners' applications systems, and comprises:

export → translation → communications → translation → import.

Testing of the individual components of each stage will normally have been thoroughly exhausted before end-to-end testing is attempted, since each partner can test each component of each stage in-house. Because of this, end-to-end testing is often wrongly confined to verification that a set of good data can flow right across the system, and really only tests the communications element. Once an EDI system nears completion, however, a more exhaustive testing schedule should be drawn up with the EDI trading partner covering as many cases as possible, which might disrupt this end-to-end flow.

It is also important at this stage to include tests for the likely volumes of data that might flow at peak times, and the average flow to be expected after, say, a year's trading. If it is planned to begin with only one partner but expect several within this period, try to persuade the partner to emulate many. This will give reassurance that expected volumes will be accommodated.

The key people responsible for testing at each end should agree a test plan and keep to it, since at this stage the tests being carried out are crucial to the success of the whole venture.

8.10   Correctness of the Business Process – Parallel Running

The final phase of testing is normally done in close co-operation with the users of the business function that is being migrated to EDI. Its aim must be to ensure that in a parallel environment, exactly the same effect is achieved by processing the EDI data as would have been achieved by the existing manual methods.

Planning for parallel running is always difficult, in that by its very nature the EDI data will arrive perhaps days before paper data. However, difficult though it may be, it is vital to check that the new process replicates the old (without, of course, the errors which EDI is intended to correct).

Where the EDI function achieves something entirely new, i.e. there was previously no comparable business function, then in place of parallel running there must be an audit team (including senior members of the business) who will compare the results of the EDI process against their system design.

8.11 Special Note – Parallel Operation

Where there is some existing EDI function, then introducing a new function must be done with care so as not to impact existing work. There are several possibilities: (Note that '✔' indicates an advantage and '✘' a disadvantage.)

- operate a test mailbox

    - ✔ keeps test environment completely separate from existing environment

    - ✘ extra cost of mailbox (but may be mitigated by negotiation)

    - ✘ partner needs to change to new EDI address for real mailbox at go-live

- use existing mailbox but differentiate by message type or test flag

    - ✔ reduced costs

    - ✘ some VANs do not allow extract by type or flag status, therefore danger of confusion with existing data

    - ✘ partner needs to change type or flag status at go-live

- rely on EDI software to route data different ways

    - ✔ no VAN issues

    - ✘ software must have this capability, and the user must be competent in its use.

There is generally less of a conflict problem when dealing with new outgoing applications or partners.

Electronic data interchange Message Development Guide

8.12 **Correct Functioning of Communications Control**

If communications are being carried out via a third-party VAN, then there will often be control functions for administering the facilities provided by the VAN, eg creating new trading relationships, obtaining reports such as postbox or mailbox lists and accounting summaries, re-extracting data after communications or internal failures, housekeeping mailboxes, etc.

These operations may be achieved by software (interactively or by sending appropriate messages) or by telephone requests to the provider. In either case, testing is necessary to gain familiarity with the environment, and to document procedures as they relate to the use made of them.

The provider will normally operate a help desk, and it is a simple matter to test how internal procedures will operate with regard to invoking this service.

Special care must be taken where more than one VAN connection is being made, either directly or through VAN interconnects (where one VAN passes messages to another for eventual delivery to the end recipient). Often the procedures and reporting capabilities differ from VAN to VAN, so in these cases testing needs to be more searching, extensive and rigorous.

Where wide area networking (eg X400, FTP) is being used, the operations of setting up and verifying routing tables, file transfers and acknowledgement mechanisms must be tested also, and the demarcations between in-house actions and WAN provider actions determined and documented.

Testing these features is important and largely independent of any other activity.

8.13 **Correctness and Completeness of Archiving and Control**

It is normal to keep copies of incoming and outgoing data for auditing purposes, and for use in case of dispute with a partner. There may also be a legal requirement to keep data for quite long periods (up to seven years for financial data).

If this falls within the EDI arena rather than elsewhere in the applications system then the correctness of the archiving subsystem and its ability to locate particular data may be more important, and should, therefore, be tested in line with its importance.

8.14 Correctness of Automation, Reporting and Error Trapping and Recovery

During the above testing, most of the error trapping and recovery routines will have been tested implicitly. It is worthwhile reviewing those elements that have not been tested and if possible setting up special conditions to test them.

Especially important when dealing with financial data are the requirements of agencies such as the Inland Revenue, who must be assured that the reporting meets their legislative requirements. EDI trading involving tax is effectively illegal without their agreement, which is not normally obtained until the necessary reports and reconciliations have been demonstrated to their inspectors.

8.15 Log File Monitoring

Post-implementation 'live-data' monitoring of the EDI messages is the final step in a testing sequence. This is important because, while EDI is more cost-effective with a high volume of messages, the effect of data errors is compounded by the volume of transactions. Checking at this stage can reduce the chance of such problems. An error that passes syntax, data validation and internal application checks will tend to stay dormant for a long while.

Errors detected at this stage are most likely to be in the meaning of the data. For example, the incorrect price may be sent back, or discount may not have been applied.

Post-implementation updating of the service agreement, although not strictly part of testing, will undoubtedly be driven by the results of testing. Has the trading partner kept to the service agreement? The agreement will probably need updating after testing and a final copy should be ready for the installation date. Assuming the testing has been a success, the system will be installed.

9 Case Studies

The following are two case studies illustrating the methods adopted by users to introduce EDI and message design in a methodical manner thus reaping the benefits of a properly structured approach.

9.1	**Case Studies 1: The National Health Service**

The following is a case study relating to the National Health Service's use of EDI. It is reproduced here with the kind permission of Mr B J Love. Although it slightly goes beyond the remit of this document in that it covers more than just pure message design, it is thought that it so well sets out the requirements, not just of the NHS but also of other prospective EDI users, that it was worth reproducing in full in this document.

**Developing National Standard Clinical EDI Messages.
B J Love**
NHS Management Executive Information Management Group, 15 Frederick Road, Birmingham B15 1JD, England

This paper presents a case study and methodology derived from the experience of the National Health Service (NHS) in England. The methodology is based on explicit ownership by clinicians of the message development process and a separation of the task of definition of information requirement from that of technical assurance and testing.

1. EDI – A definition

EDI is the transfer of structured messages, conforming to agreed standards, from one independently managed computer system to another by electronic means. The objective of EDI is to convey the minimum amount of data which will result in correct timely action with the minimum risk of error. The objective is also to free organisations from the mountains of administrative paperwork associated with exchanging information between parties involved in any business or service delivery activity. [1]

Understanding the operational requirement and agreeing the function and content of EDI messages requires active user participation. EDI is all about interaction between users who share information utilising common 'standard' messages. Agreeing the content of these messages must therefore be a group or 'community' activity. This paper describes the process of developing clinical and patient management messages leading to the adoption of national standard clinical messages for the NHS. At the outset it was necessary to provide answers to some questions often posed by doctors.

2. Who specifies the data content?

Medical EDI messages are designed to serve a practical purpose, namely to assist clinical staff to exchange the information <u>they</u> wish to share in the care of a patient. For this reason it is essential that clinicians specify the purpose, scope and content of the message.

3. Why standard messages?

A General Practitioner (GP), for example, may wish to receive EDI messages from several laboratories. A hospital may wish to exchange information with a large number of GPs. A common pre-agreed format makes the process of handling the information simpler and can also assist in avoiding errors caused by misunderstandings. If agreed standard messages are adopted, computer software suppliers are better able to produce cost effective and widely marketable applications to assist clinical staff.

4. Will doctors be obliged to use the standard messages?

Clinicians will make their own individual judgement on whether to use EDI and when and if to use a particular message. The NHS Management Executive has, however, to ensure that the option to use nationally agreed EDI messages is available to those clinical practitioners who wish to use them. It will, therefore, insist that application suppliers provide within their products the capability to handle the agreed national standard messages.

5. Which syntax standard?

The 'technical grammar' which will be used in all NHS EDI messages between NHS organisations and between the NHS and external organisations [2] is the international syntax standard UN/EDIFACT [3]. The case in support of the use of EDIFACT in healthcare has been made elsewhere [4] and its suitability for use within healthcare has been confirmed by a CEN study [5].

6. What are the priorities?

The requirement now is to secure clinical agreement to initial versions of messages identified by clinical practitioners as being of the highest priority, which are those messages which will improve links between primary and secondary care. These are; Pathology Request/Report, GP Referral and Hospital Discharge Summary, Hospital Admission Notification, Death Notification, Outpatient Attendance Report.

7. Why is there a need for a forum/mechanism for securing agreement and endorsement of each message version on behalf of the profession nationally?

A national message will only have status and credibility in the eyes of users and suppliers if it is acceptable to the professions nationally. The concept of a 'version' of a message is important. The requirements and agreed definitions of information that needs to be shared between, for example, GPs and hospital consultants, will be subject to change over time. New versions of messages will require to be agreed from time to time to reflect this. As experience of using EDI grows and it becomes very much the norm for passing information between hospitals, laboratories and GPs the contents of messages will become more refined.

8. The Process

The key objective is to establish a formal disciplined framework which achieves the alignment of clinical consultative arrangements with the matrix management process of developing National Standard Clinical EDI Messages. The stages and tasks in this process are described below.

Stage 1 Tasks – Identifying the Business Need.

Task 1 – Allocating National Priorities

Action Required – Any newly identified message requirements should be reviewed and priority allocated by formal mechanism.

Electronic data interchange Message Development Guide

Task 2 – Decision to fund/resource message development

The participation of representatives selected by the professions in messaging projects may require central 'community' funding. This might include specific training or awareness activity, preparatory work, attendance at seminars, workshops and travel and man-day payments. A critical resource constraint is the amount of time key clinician 'opinion leaders' can give.

Action Required – A 'forward look' at proposed national standard message requirements and allocation of resource.

Task 3 – Identify the communication parties

For each message or message group identify the communication parties which actively take part in the communication.

Action Required – For each message scheduled for development, identification of initial set of communication party roles.

Task 4 – Review existing relevant advisory/consultative groups

There are currently either in active or quiescent state a number of standing or ad hoc groups at the national level with specific mandates relating to information management within the NHS and associated bodies. These range from highly visible groups such as the Conference of Medical Royal Colleges Information Group to groups active within one clinical area or discipline. Groups are also active in related areas such as Social Services.

Action Required – Identify appropriate groups and contact points and make decision on how to 'channel' contacts with such groups.

Task 5 – Create appropriate EDI message 'community' advisory group

Representatives selected by the professions at the national level of each type of 'communications party' should be involved in defining the information content or confirming its relevance to current and projected information exchange data flows.

Action Required – Secure involvement of communication parties that are recognised as having the support of their peer group.

Task 6 – Identifying business requirement/potential

Task 7 – Scoping the standard message activity

Both these tasks should ideally be led by a representative of one of the major communication parties.

Action Required – Production of a description of the business processes and scope of the standard messaging activity being undertaken.

Task 8 – Review relevant existing NHS data subsets and data models

Any work undertaken in support of developing new messages should utilise other work already done on data definitions.

Action Required – Clarification of what work is ongoing. Decisions required on when and by whom work will be taken forward and whether existing groups/collaborative machinery can carry out some of the work of defining information requirements for messages.

Stage 2 – Defining Information Requirements

Task 9 – Review available and relevant EDI messages in UK and abroad.

Messaging activity (particularly in healthcare in Europe) can be a very valuable contribution to this work. Directories of ongoing EDI work are maintained by CEN TC251 [6] and by the Western European EDIFACT Board [7].

Action Required – Obtain information on relevant messaging activities.

Task 10 – Describing the Business Process (Domain Information Model (DIM))

(NB Tasks 10 (DIM), 11 (Scenarios) and 12 (GMD) correspond to the message development model being applied within CEN TC 251 (Medical Informatics) [8].) *Only* those concepts in the problem domain which need to be shared by the communication parties should be included in the model. Information related to the internal processes in an application programme should be omitted. Common concepts in healthcare may be re-used in several problem domains; but the exact attributes and operations may differ from domain to domain.

Action Required – Production of a DIM, a description of the relevant information domain. The DIM identifies the individual items or objects (people, things, concepts) that are relevant and the structured relationship between them. The DIM should also be supported by detailed information on each 'object' and its attributes.

Task 11 – Describing the Message Flows (Scenarios)

Scenarios may be regarded as substantive, concrete examples of a particular user situation. The scenario shows sequences of messages exchanged between the communication parties in the problem domain. The messages are the results of the services requested and provided by each party.

Action Required – Identification of the specific message flows required to support the business process and any dependencies, relationships between them (eg this message will be a response to another specified message). Agreement on which messages to select for development as national EDI standard messages, requirement for error/acknowledgement messages etc.

Task 12 – Identifying message level information requirement (General Message Description (GMD))

A message incorporates a selected amount of information which is exchanged between two systems for a given purpose. The GMD is a special view of the overall DIM reflecting one message type. The GMD details the objects and attributes to be conveyed in the message. At the conclusion of this task there should be agreement on the message structure but this should not include details of the specific design of the message within the EDIFACT interchange format. At this stage any extraordinary security/confidentiality requirements should be specified.

Action Required – Obtain information on relevant data exchange requirements.

Stage 3 – Establish Data Specification.

Task 13 – Mapping to existing NHS Data Dictionary/The NHS Coded Thesaurus of Clinical Terms

Task 14 – Mapping to existing coding schemes/values

Action Required – The NHS Data Dictionary/The NHS Coded Thesaurus of Clinical Terms is searched and appropriate items at data element level and at coding scheme level with relevant information on concrete presentation (number of characters, alphabetic/numeric etc.) is extracted to match the requirements of the GMD.

Task 15 – Creating New Entries in Data Dictionary/Coded Thesaurus of Clinical Terms

Task 16 – Creating New Code Values/Schemes

Action Required – Create new entries for any coding schemes/values and data element specifications required for a GMD not yet available in the NHS Data Dictionary/Coded Thesaurus of Clinical Terms.

Stage 4 – Design Messages

Task 17 – Review existing relevant EDIFACT messages in UK and abroad

Task 18 – Mapping to UN/EDIFACT data element, segment and code directories.

Task 19 – Enhancing UN/EDIFACT

Electronic data interchange Message Development Guide

The UN/EDIFACT procedures, current standard messages and data directories require amendment and continuous review to ensure that UN/EDIFACT can meet the needs of healthcare.

Action Required – Identify changes to UN/EDIFACT Directories to accommodate healthcare requirements identified. Secure agreement of Western European EDIFACT Board (WEEB) Message Development Group 9 (Healthcare) to produce proposals to amend Data Directories.

Task 20 – Select existing or structure new message format

Action Required – Fit GMD to an appropriate UN/EDIFACT structure including any security/confidentiality requirements that are to be incorporated at the message level. Quality assure EDIFACT technical structure.

Task 21 – Provide Message Implementation Guidelines (MIG)

Unambiguous and 'user friendly' guidance must be provided to explain how the user information (as defined in the GMD) is mapped to the UN/EDIFACT Message and the purpose of the message.

Action Required – Production of MIG written jointly by an EDIFACT specialist and a representative from the clinical domain which the message serves.

Stage 5 – Secure National Agreement

Task 22 – Secure agreement on national standard trial message.

Action required – Representatives of the professions involved as 'communication parties' agree on a national basis that the *information* content of the message and MIG is appropriate for the particular information exchange (business purpose). The national standard trial message is available for general use in conformance with the MIG.
Task 23 – Technical assurance of message by 'testing in use'.

Action required – Monitor experience of use of national trial message.

Task 24 – Agree National Standard Message

Action required – When 'experience in use' demonstrates fitness for purpose of message secure endorsement from Clinicians as National Standard Message. Consult with suppliers about timetable for implementing national standard message.

Stage 6 – Maintain Standard Messages (Change Control)

Task 25 – Update National Standard Messages

Any message will have a lifecycle determined by the business needs of the NHS. Messages are allocated version numbers to enable effective change control as they develop in line with changing information exchange requirements. It is expected that simple versions of messages will be implemented initially with later versions reflecting the pace at which the clinical community achieves agreement on common definitions, structures, coding schemes etc.

Action Required – To monitor changes in requirements and manage changes through the process.

[1] 'An Information Management and Technology Strategy for the NHS in England – Exchanging Healthcare Messages with EDI.' Department of Health 1992.

[2] Department of Health London. Executive Letter EL (92) 34. Adoption of UN/EDIFACT as the NHS Standard for Electronic Data Interchange of structured messages 1992.

[3] ISO 9735 (EN 29735) Electronic Data Interchange for administration commerce and transport (EDIFACT) Application syntax rules.

[4] Love B – UN/EDIFACT – an EDI standard for Health Care in *Progress in Standardisation in Health*

Care Informatics. De Moor G, McDonald C, Noothoven Van Goor J (eds) IOS Press 1993: 156–161.

[5] 'CEN Technical Report CR 1350 : 1993' Investigation of Syntaxes for existing Interchange Formats to be used in Health Care.

[6] CEN Technical Committee 251. Directory of the European Standardisation Requirements for Health Care Informatics and Programme for the Development of Standards. Version 1.7 June 1993.

[7] Western European EDIFACT Board Message Development Group (MD9) Healthcare 'Introduction'.

[8] CEN TC251 Messages for Exchange of Clinical Laboratory Information. First working document October 1993.

9.2 Case Studies 2: Migration of Education Proprietary Standards to UN/EDIFACT. (MEPS project)

This case study differs from the previous one in that messages already exist in this sector and so the business data mapping had already taken place. There were, however, many different non-compatible standards being used to carry similar data. This project was designed to bring the standards together and produce common messages in the EDIFACT syntax.

9.2.1 Background

The various groups in the education sector had designed, and were using, structured data records to exchange information such as student records and examination results, between organisations. Until this project was started there was little incentive to standardise the format of those records. Organisations, such as the Department for Education and the Environment, which received information from many different types of organisation, were forced to accept many diverse forms of message with broadly similar content. Some of these messages were based on EDIFACT syntax, though they had not been rigorously tested by being submitted to the standards process, but most were completely proprietary.

Against this background of incompatibility, the EDI Association's Education Sector Interest Section (ESIS) now part of the Public Sector Interest Section (PSIS) applied for and got EU TEDIS funding towards creating EDIFACT messages. This was intended to bring together all partners in Education to use a common method of transferring data and reduce overall costs in the sector. As a secondary benefit, these messages would be put to UN/EDIFACT for standardisation and, therefore, European Union and international use.

An independent consultant, André Bottin (Enterprise AB) was contracted to lead the project and actually do most of the design work, with technical assistance from the EDIA. The partners in the project were the DFEE, Business and Technology Education Council (BTEC), International Baccalaureate Organisation (IBO), The UK Academic Examination Boards, EDIFrance and Enterprise AB.

9.2.2 Getting Started

As the messages already existed, the identification of data requirements was simplified. Examples of all the existing message specifications were collected, together with the specification of ANSI Transaction set 130, used for similar purposes. The ANSI messages were for national use, and there were no plans to convert them to EDIFACT. The US education sector has a working system and had no plans to extend its use beyond its borders. The Pan-American Education message design group was very supportive of the project and provided the MEPS team with help and encouragement. A search revealed that, apart from the Americans, no one else was working on education messages, so the project had a green field to work in.

9.2.3 The Data Model

There were many different messages from each group with much overlapping functionality. The ANSI and BTEC board's messages seemed to contain most of the functionality required and a shortlist of five messages was decided upon. When analysing the data in greater detail, however, it was found that the set could be reduced to three messages by combing three messages into one. There were messages for enrolling for examinations, for reporting grades from examination centres and for reporting exam results. By logically separating two segment groups containing the bulk or detailed information and making them mutually exclusive the ENROLM or enrolment message could be used for all three cases.

The reason for this approach was that many details were common to both types of message, for example, originating and destination organisations' details, and it was a recognition of the EDIFACT philosophy of generality of purpose of messages. The advantage was a reduction in effort and time in designing them because much was reused. A secondary objective was to ease the process of getting them through the standards process by reducing the number of messages to be submitted. Much of the design process was bottom-up, in that the basic functionality and data entities were given, because these were a replacement for existing messages. To aid in this, a decision to use only existing EDIFACT data objects was taken. This is not really a problem now because many thousands of objects have been defined in the past, so finding a match is not too difficult. A few years ago this might have been a problem, and much more work would have been required to design objects from scratch. The messages themselves and the segment groups are unique to MEPS, but every other object was reused.

Finally, data qualifier code values had to be chosen so that qualified generic data objects took on a specific meaning. Values were used from existing code lists where it was thought the meaning was correct, but this is a notoriously difficult area as the semantics of code value names can be unclear and descriptive text often less than useful. Many code values are described as 'Self-explanatory' when they most definitely are not to anyone outside the original design team.

9.2.4 Designing the messages

Each existing message was analysed and a matrix created of data objects and their semantics. Often identical objects might have different names (eg Pupil Name and Student Name) and different sizes. This exercise filtered the data into a set of identically named and sized objects. This was not a simple desk exercise. The parties involved in the use of these messages had to be consulted in case the meaning had been misconstrued. This was perhaps the most time consuming aspect of the message design.

The next stage was to group data into the highest level object – the message – which met the data requirements of each user organisation. Having determined this and agreed it with the user organisations, the data was again filtered by logically grouping into hierarchical data entities which equated to segment groups, segments, composite data elements and simple data elements. Some of this work was eased because the BTEC messages, for example, were already using EDIFACT data objects.

Like all design, this was an iterative process. For example, the Name and Address segment (NAD) was to be used throughout for party information, even where only the name was required, as is common in EDIFACT messages, but this was changed when it became evident that the NAD was likely to be phased out for new

Electronic data interchange Message Development Guide

message design, in favour of Party NAme segment (PNA) and the ADdRess segment. (ADR) By replacing NAD with PNA and ADR, some efficiencies were realised. Often the address was not required, so PNA on its own could be used. In other cases one party could have several addresses, so the ADR could repeat for a single PNA.

The design was also changed several times when possible segment collisions were detected, so the structure had to be re-thought to avoid it. Finally three messages: STUREC, ENROLM and PRGDAT were produced.

9.2.5 Documentation

At all design stages, a message documentation tool, EDI-TIE's Documentation Manager, was used. This contains the EDIFACT directories, so reduces the amount of data entry required, and prints out the branching diagrams and message documentation in the EDIFACT standard form for submitting with a Data Maintenance Request (DMR).

9.2.6 Submitting to UN/EDIFACT

Before the DMRs can be put forward for status 0, they must be presented by the sponsoring organisation, the EDIA's ESIS group, to the relevant message design (MD) group. As these messages are, in reality, national messages, though designed using international standards, agreement has to be reached in the MD group that they meet the regional and international need. One small problem was the lack of an education MD group! This was solved by forming a sub-group to the Public Administration MD group. At the time of writing this group was considering the messages, but no major hurdles are expected.

When satisfied that the messages meet business requirements, they will be submitted to the regional TAGs as DMR New Message Requests. Once all TAGs have accepted the messages as being technically correct, they are published at Status 1 for trial use. Implementations will then turn up any problems not found before and the messages can be reworked and submitted for Status 2.

Finally, The partners in the design process have to commit to using the new messages and show to their business managers that the benefits forecast have been realised.

Annex A: Glossary

Term	Explanation
Alphabetic	Characters from the sets a–z and A–Z
Alphanumeric	The characters a–z, A–Z and numbers 0–9, plus punctuation. In *EDIFACT* characters used in service segments are defined by the level A subset of ISO 646, but character encoding for user data is not specified.
ANA	The Article Number Association. Responsible for the Tradacoms EDI standard.
ANSI	The American National Standards Institute.
ANSI X12	The American national standard for EDI.
Batch EDI	As opposed to *Interactive EDI*, the building up of an interchange containing one or more messages, and sending it by message switching or file transfer to the recipient in a one-way transfer. The now accepted term for traditional EDI using these techniques.
BIM	Business Information Modelling group. A UN/EDIFACT group investigating standard ways of modelling and representing business data requirements.
Bridge	The link between a BSU and its related unit(s) of information in a given *directory*.
BSI	The British Standards Institution.
BSR	Basic Semantic Repository. The directory for *BSU's*.
BSU	Basic Semantic Units. Data entities uniquely defined in terms of their use in the business environment.
CEN	the Comité Européen de Normalisation (Committee for European Standardisation). Responsible for harmonising European nations' standards. Now responsible for European EDIFACT standards making body *EBES*.
Code sets	The set of coded values associated with a coded *simple data element*.
Component data element	*A simple data element used within a composite data element.*
Composite data element	A logical grouping of *simple data elements*.
Conditional	A type of status describing *data objects* that may be omitted under certain conditions. Synonymous with 'optional' in many cases.
Data dictionary	A definitive *directory of data objects* upon which other directories are based.
DMR	Data Maintenance Request. Standard mechanism for submitting new or modified data objects into the *UN/EDIFACT* process.

Electronic data interchange Message Development Guide

Data objects	Logical parcels of meaningful information, upon which actions can be taken. In EDI this includes the *simple data element*, *composite data element*, *segment*, *segment group* and *message*.
Directory	A collection of *data objects*.
EBES	European Board for EDI Standards. The *CEN* administered replacement for *UN/ECE* Western European EDIFACT Board (WEEB).
ECA	The Electronic Commerce Association, The UK trade association for users, suppliers and consultants involved in Electronic Commerce. Formerly The *EDI Association*.
EDI	Electronic Data Interchange. The recognised standard method of passing structured business and administrative data between trading partners.
EDI interrupts.	Colloquial term used to indicate a system in which the EDI process requires human intervention, such as the re-keying of data, to complete.
EDIA	The EDI Association. The UK trade association for users, suppliers and consultants involved in EDI. Now broadened in scope and relaunched as the Electronic Commerce Association (ECA).
EDIFACT	Electronic Data Interchange for Administration, Commerce and Transport. The *ISO* standard for EDI. See also UN/EDIFACT.
Electronic Commerce	The use of electronic means of machine intercommunication for business and administration. It includes *EDI*, Electronic Funds Transfer and commercial *internet* trading systems.
EWOS	The European Workshop for Open Systems. A group involved in the promotion of Open Systems in all areas of *electronic commerce*, including EDI.
Http	HyperText Transfer Protocol. The protocol of the *World Wide Web*, often seen in *URL's*.
Identifier	A *data element* used to identify a data object.
Interactive EDI (I-EDI)	A method of using EDI structured data between co-operating machines in a dialogue. Required where fast response times are needed, and the result of a query or command may affect the subsequent course of the transaction.
Internet	An international collection of interconnected academic, government and commercial networks, characterised by their use of TCP/IP protocols, which allow open global communications at very cheap rates. Expected to become an important carrier of EDI in the near future.

ISO	International Organization for Standardization. The organisation that publishes International standards, including the *EDIFACT syntax*.
Locodes	Standard international codes for places. Comprised of the ISO country code and a national or industry place code. Part of the *TDED*.
Mandatory	An adjective indicating that a data object must be present if its containing data object is present, for example, a mandatory segment must be present if the segment group containing it is present.
MDG	Message Design Guidelines. A formal, generic, set of rules used by message designers to ensure compliance of their messages.
Message	In EDI an electronic 'document'; a collection of *segment groups*, *segments*, and *data elements* that together fulfil a business requirement, eg an invoice, order or price list. Synonymous with the ANSI Transaction Set
Message directory	A collection of *messages* and their inclusive *data objects* that can be used for commerce and administration. In UN/EDIFACT they are given a status, a date and release, eg D.93A is Draft 1993 *directory* release A.
Message Implementation Guidelines (MIG's)	Message implementation guidelines. A formal document that lays out rules for the use of a particular message and its contained data objects under specified conditions.
Numeric	Characters from the set 0–9.
Odette	Organisation for Data Exchange by Tele-Transmission in Europe. European EDI standards body for the automotive industry.
Qualifier	*A simple data element* that gives specific meaning to the generic *data object* associated with it.
Re-usability	The ability to use *data objects* without having to design new versions.
Responsible agency	An organisation, such as ISO, IATA or the UN, which administers *code lists*.
Scenarios	A description of the business or administrative process in which *electronic commerce* takes place.
Segment	A logical grouping of *composite* and *stand-alone data elements*. Identified by its *segment tag*
Segment collision	A message design pitfall where repeating *segments* of the same type are separated by other *conditional segments* and, therefore, cannot be identified correctly when those *conditional segments* are not present.
Segment group	A logical grouping of *segments* and other segment groups.

Segment Tag	A three-letter string that identifies the segment type.
Simple data element	The smallest unit of meaningful data in EDI. Can be *stand-alone* or a *component of a composite data element*.
SITPRO	Simpler Trade Procedures Board. Until January 1996, the organisation responsible for providing UK input to the *EDIFACT* standards making process, and with promoting the use of those standards. This rôle has moved to *UKCEDIS*, administered by the *ECA*.
SSADM	Structured Systems Analysis & Design Methodology. The recommended methodology for government projects.
Stand-alone	Adjective applied to *data objects* that are not grouped with other *data objects* at the same level.
Syntax	The rules describing the format and structure of *EDI data objects*, independently of the semantics.
TAG	Technical Assessment Group. A group of experts responsible for testing new *data objects* for conformity to *syntax* and *message design guideline* rules. There are several regional TAG's and one joint TAG in the *UN/EDIFACT* process.
TAG checklists	Technical Assessment Group Checklist. A distillation of the rules from the message design guidelines and other *UN/ECE* documentation.
TDED	Trade Data Elements Directory. *UN/ECE directory* of the basic *simple data element* building blocks.
TDID	Trade Data Interchange Directory. A collection of UN/ECE documents and *directories* for use in *UN/EDIFACT*.
Tradacoms	UK national *EDI* standard based on *UN/GTDI*.
Trigger segment	*A mandatory segment* placed at the beginning of every *segment group* to identify and delimit the group.
UKCEDIS	The UK Confederation for EDI Standards. A joint committee of the ANA, APACS, BINA, the *ECA* and *SITPRO*, tasked with overseeing the UK input to the *EDIFACT* standards process.
UN/ECE	United Nations Economic Commission for Europe.
UN/EDIFACT	*UN/ECE* rules for Electronic Data Interchange for Administration, Commerce and Transport. Also simply known as EDIFACT.
UNCID Rules	Uniform Rules Of Conduct For Interchange Of Trade Data By Teletransmission.
UN/GTDI	United Nations Guidelines for Trade Data Interchange. The old *UN/ECE* EDI standard.

Annex A
Glossary

UNSM	United Nations Standard Message. *A message* that has reached status 2 and been published in a *message directory* by the *UN/ECE*.
URL	Universal Resource Locator. A standard way of identifying a resource on the internet. It is constructed thus: protocol://location/filename where protocol indicates *http* for WWW pages
WWW	The World Wide Web. A logical network overlaying the *internet*. It uses the *http* protocol to carry marked-up text. It is a useful source of standards documents, and is likely to become a front-end to EDI systems.

Annex B: Contacts

Central Computer and Telecommunications Agency
CCTA
Information Interchange Branch
Rosebery Court
St Andrews Business Park
Norwich
NR7 0HS
Tel: 01603 704561   Fax: 01603 704817

Electronic Commerce Association
(Formerly the EDI Association)
Ramillies House
1-9 Hills Place
London
W1R 1AG
Tel: 0171 432 2515   Fax: 0171 432 2501

Article Number Association
11 Kingsway
London
WC2B 6AR
Tel: 0171 240 2874   Fax: 0171 240 8149

SITPRO
Venture House
29 Glasshouse Street
London
W1R 5RG
Tel: 0171 287 3525   Fax: 0171 287 5751

Annex C: STATAC Message

(Reproduced with the permission of SITPRO)

UN/EDIFACT

DRAFT RECOMMENDATION

Statement of account message

This message is available for formal trial for at least six months from the date of approval by UN/ECE/TRADE/WP.4

Organisations are invited to trial this message. Comments on the results from the trial should be forwarded to their Rapporteur's Team Secretariat as soon as they are available. Based on the results of the trials, a UNSM may be issued.

The segments, composite data elements, data elements and codes for use in the trial of this message are contained in the Draft directory. However, this information may differ from that in the Standard directory (UNTDID), even for material having the same identifying tags.

Message Type	: STATAC
Version	: D
Release	: 95A
Contr. Agency	: UN
Status	: 2
Revision	: 1
Date	: 95-01-06

SOURCE: Joint Statistics Group (JM8)

Electronic data interchange Message Development Guide

CONTENTS
Statement of account message

0. INTRODUCTION

1. SCOPE

    1.1 Functional definition

    1.2 Field of application

    1.3 Principles

2. REFERENCES

3. TERMS AND DEFINITIONS

4. MESSAGE DEFINITION

    4.1 Data segment clarification

        4.1.1 Header section

        4.1.2 Detail section

        4.1.3 Summary section

    4.2 Data segment index (alphabetical sequence)

    4.3 Message structure

        4.3.1 Segment table

For general information on UN standard message types see UN Trade Data Interchange Directory, UNTDID, Part 4, Section 2.6, UN/ECE UNSM

General Introduction

0. INTRODUCTION

This specification provides the definition of the Statement of account message (STATAC) to be used in Electronic Data Interchange (EDI) between trading partners involved in administration, commerce and transport.

1. SCOPE

   1.1 Function Definition

   A statement of Account is a communication from a Seller or his agent to a Buyer or his agent, providing information about the status of an account at a specific point in time. It is used as an aid to reconciliation. At the same time it may be a reminder of payment due.

   1.2 Field of Application

   The UN Standard Statement of Account Message may be used for both national and international business. It is based on universal commercial practice and is not dependent on the type of business or industry.

   1.3 Principles

   - A statement of Account may refer to only one account, in one currency.

   - A statement of Account contains only outstanding debts and does not specify any debts which have been cleared since the previous Statement.

– A Statement of Account may be initiated at any time by the Seller, depending upon agreement between the Buyer and the Seller.

2. REFERENCES

See UNTDID, Part 4, Chapter 2.6 UN/ECE UNSM – General Introduction, Section 1.

3. TERMS AND DEFINITIONS

See UNTDID, Part 4, Chapter 2.6 UN/ECE UNSM – General Introduction, Section 2.

4. MESSAGE DEFINITION

4.1 Data Segment Clarification

– This section should be read in conjunction with the Branching Diagram and the Segment Table which indicate mandatory, conditional and repeating requirements.

– The following guidelines and principles apply to the whole message and are intended to facilitate the understanding and implementation of the message:

– All specified dates/times should be in the format 'yymmdd'/'hhmm' unless all parties involved in the transaction agree that there is a functional requirement for an alternative format. Periods should be specified as whole numbers representing the required period as indicated in the format qualifier (weeks, months, etc.)

– Where a choice of code or text is given only the code element should be used wherever possible.

– Conditional data that is not required in the message should not be included.

- Care must be taken that the segment qualifier in dependent segments do not conflict with the segment qualifier of the trigger segment of a group.

- Free text information within the message should be avoided as this inhibits automatic processing. It is only used when additional information that cannot be accommodated within the other segments is required.

4.1.1   Header section

Information to be provided in the Header section:

0010   1 UNH, Message header
A service segment starting and uniquely identifying a message. The message type code for the Statement of account message is STATAC.

Note: Statement of account messages conforming to this document must contain the following data in segment UNH, composite S009:

Data element   0065 STATAC
                0052 D
                0054 95A
                0051 UN

0020   BGM, Beginning of message
A segment by which the sender must uniquely identify the Statement of Account.

0030   DTM, Date/time/period
A segment specifying the dates, and when relevant, the times related to the whole message. The segment must be specified at least once to specify the message date as allocated by the sender.

0040   RFF, Reference
       A segment for referencing documents which relate to the whole message.

0050   CUX, Currencies
       A segment identifying the currency of the Statement of Account. The payment currency is the default currency for all amounts, it must be specified in international transactions.

0060   Segment group 1: NAD-SG2
       A group of segments identifying the parties involved in the transaction and, optionally the contact points and numbers.

0070   NAD, Name and address
       A segment to identify a party name and address, either by coded identification or in clear form.

0080   Segment group 2: CTA-COM
       A group of segments identifying the contact person or department for a trading party and specifying the communication channel and number.

0090   CTA, Contact information
       A segment to identify a person or department and their function, to whom communications should be directed.

0100   COM, Communication contact
       A segment specifying the communications channel and number for the specified contact.

4.1.2 Detail section

       Information to be provided in the Detail section:

0110 Segment group 3: DOC-MOA-DTM-RFF
A group of segments providing details of all documents, eg invoices, credit notes, etc, to which the Statement of Account refers. It contains details of the monetary values associated with the documents and of relevant dates. There must be at least one occurrence of this group within the Statement of Account Message.

0120 DOC, Document/message details
A segment identifying the reference document against which payment is to be made.

0130 MOA, Monetary amount
A segment to specify the required amounts for the referenced document eg amount due, discount amount, payment amount.

0140 DTM, Date/time/period
A segment to specify the date of the referenced document and to indicate any other relevant dates applicable, eg Due date, Tax point date, etc.

0150 RFF, Reference
A segment for the inclusion of any additional references related to the reference document.

4.1.3 Summary section

Information to be provided in the Summary section:

0160 UNS, Section control
A service segment placed at the start of the summary section to avoid segment collision.

Electronic data interchange Message Development Guide

0170 MOA, Monetary amount
A segment specifying the total amount pertaining to the message. The outstanding balance amount is mandatory and is taken as given, ie it is not subject to recalculation.

0180 FTX, Free text
A segment for free text information, in coded or clear form.

0190 UNT, Message trailer
A service segment ending a message, giving the total number of segments in the message and the control reference number of the message.

4.2 Data segment index (Alphabetical sequence by tag)

BGM Beginning of message
COM Communication contact
CTA Contact information
CUX Currencies
DOC Document/message details
DTM Date/time/period
FTX Free text
MOA Monetary amount
NAD Name and address
RFF Reference
UNH Message header
UNS Section control
UNT Message trailer

4.3 Message structure

4.3.1 Segment table

Pos Tag Name   S   R

HEADER SECTION

0010 UNH Message header   M   1
0020 BGM Beginning of message   M   1
0030 DTM Date/time/period   M   5

Annex C
STATAC Message

```
0040   RFF Reference                    C   5
0050   CUX Currencies                   C   1

0060   ──── Segment group1 ────         M   5────+
0070   NAD Name and address             M   1      │
                                                   │
0080   ──── Segment group2 ────         C   5──+ │
0090   CTA Contact information          M   1
0100   COM Communication contact        C   5── +
```

DETAIL SECTION

```
0110   ──── Segment group 3             M   200000 ─+
0120   DOC Document/message
       details                          M   1        │
0130   MOA Monetary/amount              M   5        │
0140   DTM Date/time/period             C   5        │
0150   RFF Reference                    C   5 ─────+
```

SUMMARY SECTION

```
0160   UNS Section control              M   1
0170   MOA Monetary amount              M   5
0180   FTX Free text                    C   5
0190   UNT Message trailer              M   1
```

Annex D: EDI and VAT

This is a subsection of a larger document 'HM Customs & Excise guidance on EDI usage' which is reproduced in full in the EDI Implementation Guide *in the same series.*

THE REQUIREMENTS REGARDING COMPUTER DATA INTERCHANGE OF INVOICE FOR VALUE ADDED TAX PURPOSES IN THE UNITED KINGDOM

A guidance note as supplied to trade organisations by Her Majesty's Customs and Excise

The Law requires:

Notice of Intention
Before any system for transmitting tax invoices can be accepted as operational, each organisation involved must give the Commissioners of Customs and Excise at least one month's notice in writing. This should be sent to the local VAT office. It should be borne in mind that the longer the period of notice, then the greater the time that will be available to sort out any problems.

Compliance with Requirements
The organisations involved must comply with the Requirements imposed by the Commissioners of Customs and Excise. Please note that these requirements may be amended or supplemented from time to time.

The Requirements – A Summary of the Conditions Imposed by the Department

System Trials
The parties concerned must first trial the system and provide Customs and Excise with the opportunity of attending one or more of these trials to observe the trial and inspect the results.

System Changes
Any significant change in the system such as a change from exchange on magnetic tape to exchange via electronic mail system, or a major change in the computerised accounting system which produces the

invoice information, must be advised to Customs and Excise at least one month before implementation. Again, the earlier, the better.

Control Information and Reports

The Sender
For each invoice file created for transmission purposes, the sender must produce a control document on paper for retention in his records. This must show, among other things:

(a) the full name and address of the recipient of the invoice file and the sender's name, address and VAT registration number;

(b) the unique transmission reference (see paragraph 4), or other unique reference allocated to the invoice file, and the transmission date;

(c) the total numbers and types of invoices (or other documents) on the file;

(d) for each tax rate, the total tax exclusive value of supplies mentioned in the file;

(e) the total tax charged at each rate on the above; and

(f) the total value of any exempt supplies in the file.

All the above information must also be included as control data within the transmitted invoice file and provided that the receiver can fulfil certain other requirements, a copy of the control document need not be sent to the recipient.

The Receiver
On receipt of a transmission, the file will be deformatted from the transmission message standard to the installation's own transaction file format.

The data and values at (g) and (f) in paragraph 3.1 must be printed out on a control report. The values at paragraph 3.1 (c)–(f) must now be re-calculated by totalling the relevant values from the invoice file at

Annex D
EDI and VAT

transaction level again the calculated totals must be printed out. Providing the two sets of values agree exactly, then the file may be processed normally as purchase invoices received. If, however, a discrepancy is identified at this stage, then the file must be rejected (either partly or wholly) and a copy of the control/discrepancy report(s) must be forwarded to the sender to take corrective action. Copies of all control and discrepancy reports must be retained as part of the business records.

If, for technical reasons, it is not possible to receive or read a transmission, then the transmission may be treated as not received and a control document need not be raised. The sender should, of course, be advised to re-transmit.

If, for any other reason, it is not possible to read and print the control information at para 3.1 (a)–(f) but the file is accepted for processing, a copy of the sender's control document must be obtained and the control totals thereon verified by totalling the requisite values at invoice transaction level.

Unique Identification of Invoice Files
Each invoice file must be uniquely identified by data within the transmission. This identification is usually the generation and version number of the file related to the customer and supplier details. The sender will normally maintain a discrete generation number series for each customer, the generation number being incremented by one for each file transmitted. Installations are, of course, free to agree on some other suitably unique identification if they so choose.

Monitoring to Ensure no Duplication
The recipient of an invoice file must set up a system which will detect and report the receipt of a duplicated transmission. The monitoring of the generation number and version number series would seem to be a suitable method for most systems, but, an additional control on the value of transmission files received could also be used. This should provide:

Electronic data interchange Message Development Guide

(a) a control to ensure that all invoice files transmitted have been received; and

(b) an appropriate means of identifying a duplicate invoice file.

Provision of Evidence (in accordance with Section 5(4) of Civil Evidence Act 1968/Law Reform (Miscellaneous Provisions) (Scotland) Act 1948)

You must provide, or arrange for the provision of a certificate in accordance with section 5(4) of the Civil Evidence Act 1968 should this be requested by Customs and Excise.

Computer Bureau Services
If using a computer bureau or similar organisation for any part of the procedure, then an undertaking must be obtained that the company involved:

(a) is aware that the provisions of the Finance Act 1985, Section 10, apply in respect of any computer used for such purposes; and

(b) will provide a certification in accordance with Section 5(4) of the Civil Evidence Act 1968 if so required by the Commissioners.

Names and Addresses on Invoices
The full name and address and VAT registration number of the supplier and the full name and address of the receiver may be recorded once per invoice file, eg; in the trader record, provided all the conditions are met in full.

Alternatively to 8 – Shortened Names and Addresses may be shown on each Invoice Record
Providing Customs and Excise have been given prior notice, the name and address records may be reduced, eg; to a shortened version of the name and full post cost on condition that:

(a) the file control report shows the full names and addresses; and

(b) the same shortened version must not be used by two or more companies separately registered for VAT or re-allocated to another user.

Preservation of Documents and Audit Trail
You must retain copies of all documents related to a particular transmitted file for the statutory period required by VAT legislation unless a shorter period has been approved by the local VAT office.

For the relevant Scottish or Northern Ireland legislation where applicable.

The historic record of the invoice data must contain all the invoice details and may be stored on paper magnetic media or similar or on microfilm. It is desirable from an audit viewpoint that where possible a record of the constitution of the file at transaction level be maintained.

For instance the constitution of the transmitted file may be recorded within summary reports, eg a listing of invoice numbers, values, etc, associated with the unique file reference or the invoice records are retained in such a way that the transmitted file content can be reproduced either manually or on magnetic media for audit purposes.

Changes in Requirements
In order to meet changes in legislation, or in order to make changes found to be necessary in the light of experience, the Commissioners of Customs and Excise reserve the right to amend or change these requirements as they see fit.

Bibliography

The EDIFACT Standards; John Berge, NCC Blackwell, 2nd edition 1995.

Business and Information Modelling Framework for UN/EDIFACT; UN/EDIFACT BIM group 1995

EDI Implementation Guide; CCTA, published by HMSO 1996, ISBN 0 11 330 842 6

EDI Security: A User Friendly Guide for Business Managers; EDI Association and Axiom Services Ltd. 1994

Electronic Data Interchange in Government: The Business Opportunities; CCTA, 1994

Message version/release rules, TRADE/WP.4/R.601; UN/ECE, 31 July 1989

Message version/release rules, TRADE/WP.4/R.720; UN/ECE, 14 December 1990

Structured Systems Analysis and Design Methodology, G Cutts; Paradigm, 1988

The Trade Data Elements Directory; UN/ECE, 1993

Trade Data Interchange Directory – ISO 7372; ISO

UN/EDIFACT message design guidelines – TRADE/WP.4/R.840/Rev.2; UN/ECE, 1994

UN/EDIFACT Rules for Presentation of Standardised Message and Directories Documentation TRADE/WP.4/R.1023/Rev.2; UN/ECE, 1994

UN/EDIFACT syntax rules – ISO 9735; ISO, 1996

Uniform Rules of Conduct for Interchange of Trade Data by Teletransmission; UN/ECE